Love It Don't Leave It

26 Ways to Get What You Want at Work

Beverly Kaye and Sharon Jordan-Evans

16
EasyRead Large

RHYW

Copyright Page from the Original Book

Love It, Don't Leave It

Berrett-Koehler Publishers, Inc.
235 Montgomery Street, Suite 650
San Francisco, California 94104-2916
Tel: (415) 288-0260, Fax: (415) 362-2512
www.bkconnection.com

Ordering information for print editions
Quantity sales. Special discounts are available on quantity purchases by corporations, associations, and others. For details, contact the "Special Sales Department" at the Berrett-Koehler address above.
Individual sales. Berrett-Koehler publications are available through most bookstores. They can also be ordered directly from Berrett-Koehler: Tel: (800) 929-2929; Fax: (802) 864-7626; www.bkconnection.com
Orders for college textbook/course adoption use. Please contact Berrett-Koehler: Tel: (800) 929-2929; Fax: (802) 864-7626.
Orders by U.S. trade bookstores and wholesalers. Please contact Ingram Publisher Services, Tel: (800) 509-4887; Fax: (800) 838-1149; E-mail: customer.service@ingrampublisherservices.com; or visit www.ingrampublisherservices.com/Ordering for details about electronic ordering.

First Edition
Paperback print edition ISBN 978-1-57675-250-0
PDF e-book ISBN 978-1-57675-875-5

2008-1

Book production management by Michael Bass Associates. Cover design and illustrations by Tracy Rocca.

Set in 16 pt. Verdana

TABLE OF CONTENTS

WE CANNOT
DIRECT
THE WIND—
BUT WE CAN
ADJUST
OUR SAILS.

Praise for Love It, Don't Leave It

***"Love It, Don't Leave It** is a must-read for all those who want to take control of their performance and their careers despite today's uncertainties. The employee is an active agent, charged with knowing him or herself well enough to find the right role, set the right expectations, build the right relationships, and so forge the right career. In their immensely practical book, Kaye and Jordan-Evans show how."*

—**Marcus Buckingham,** coauthor of *First, Break All the Rules* and *Now, Discover Your* Strengths.

***

"Finally, a handbook for taking action that every employee needs and any employee can use to take ownership and accountability for their job, career and happiness. When you're tired of playing 'the blame game' and want to get results, pick up this book!"

—**Bob Nelson,** Ph.D., author of *1001 Ways to Reward Employees* and *1001 Ways to Take Initiative at Work*

***

"This book is a rich buffet of ideas for taking your work to the next level. I savored this wise and witty book from cover to cover. Every reader should dip in with gusto!"

—Dick Leider, couthor of *Whistle While You Work*

***

"This is not just another 'fix-me-because-I'm-broken' book, or worse, 'Take this job and shove it!' Instead, the authors succeed with sensitivity, wisdom and wit, in offering real solutions that put employees with workplace woes in the driver's seat. The reader is invited to make assertive choices from a menu chock full of practical know-how and is inspired to put those choices into action."

—Stanlee Phelps, master coach and author of *The Assertive Woman*

***

"Kaye and Jordan-Evans have done it again—hard-hitting, practical advice on how to bloom where you are planted. Before you find a greener pasture, let them show you how to mow the grass."

—**John Izzo,** author of *Awakening Corporate Soul*

***

"Bev and Sharon have the gift of serving both the interests of employee and the institution in the same breath. This book offers another important step in creating workplaces which contain both commitment and humanity."

—**Peter Block,** author of *Flawless Consulting, Stewardship* and *The Answer to How Is Yes*

***

"This book is full of truth and wisdom. Many people who leave the place where they worked end up wishing they hadn't. But they left because they couldn't figure out how to get what they need there. Too bad they didn't read* Love It, Don't Leave It!** ***It would have showed them how to stay put AND find what they were looking for."

—**Bill Bridges,** author of *JobShift: How to Prosper in a Workplace Without Jobs* and *Creating You and Company: How to Think Like the CEO of Your Own Career*

***

"For the millions of workers feeling trapped in cubicle-land, this book is a godsend. Chock full of real-world advice from real employees, every page has proven strategies that can make your life at work more pleasurable and infinitely more fulfilling. If you're going to spend more time at work than at anything else you do, why not make it work for you? Read this book and find out how."

—**Charles Decker,** coauthor of *Beans: Four Principles for Running a Business in Good Times or Bad*

To my parents, Mollie and Abe, who first taught me the meaning of love, and continue (at the proud ages of eighty-seven and eighty-nine) to teach its nuances.

—Bev

And, at the other end of the spectrum...

To my first granddaughter, Emma, who lights up my life with her smile and reminds me to believe in the fundamental goodness of people.

—Sharon

Use this as a road map for your reading. After "Ask" and "Buck," read all the chapters that jump out at you, in any order. Then read "Zenith." And if there's even a remote chance you might leave, check our final chapter.

PREFACE

To: Anyone Who Works
From: Bev and Sharon

Do you ever think work would be great *if only:*

- you had more career choices?
- you had more time with your family?
- you were paid more?
- you didn't work with a jerk?
- you weren't so bored?
- you had unlimited access to chocolate?

Do you ever think the grass must be greener somewhere else? Well, you're not alone.

Too many people leave their jobs because something is wrong, or something is missing. They leave physically, by walking out the door. Or, they leave psychologically, by withdrawing their energy and commitment but staying put. And later, many regret their departures (of both kinds).

What if there were another option? What if it were possible to achieve or regain love for your work? (And we do mean love, not just like.) What if your work were something you looked forward to each day? What if it tapped your enthusiasm? Used your creativity? Made you feel appreciated? (Are you thinking, "Fat chance?") But, really, what if work could truly deliver the goods? We think it can.

Workplace satisfaction is a two-way street. Yes, it demands effort from your manager and from the leaders of your organization. (We wrote our previous books based on that premise.) But it also demands initiative and effort from you.

We believe, quite passionately, that positive change is not only possible but well worth your effort. We feel certain that with a few well-chosen steps, you can get more of what you want, right where you are.

We asked over fifteen thousand people why they stayed in their organizations. The top five stay factors across all industries were:

- exciting, challenging work;
- a chance to learn and grow;
- great people to work with;
- fair pay; and
- a great boss.

Which of those factors matters most to you? Which would you like a little more of? We hope this book will make "getting it" a little easier.

We've based the hints, tips, and tools you'll find throughout the book on our research and our interactions with thousands of working people worldwide. You'll also find five key messages woven throughout the chapters:

What you want could be found right where you are. Perhaps all you need to do is get clear about what's missing and go after it. Look inside before you jump outside. Master the art and science of asking for what you want.

You're in charge. You are ultimately responsible for your own workplace satisfaction. Don't expect your manager to be a mind reader or your organization to be solely responsible for your happiness. Others do have a role to play. But the bottom line is, you're in control, and it's up to you to fix what's wrong or find what's missing.

There are (at least) twenty-six ways to take the initiative. Of course, there are different strokes for different folks. That's why we've identified dozens of potential action steps. We've arranged them alphabetically, all for your consideration.

Don't wait. That "lovin' feeling" may not find you. You may have to find it! Instead of "settling" for work that doesn't work for you, take steps now to improve it. Don't wait for someone else to take the first step.

Double-check those greener pastures. Too often we leave for greener pastures elsewhere only to find Astroturf. The new workplace may have the same, or different (sometimes even worse), challenges, frustrations, and disappointments. Check it out before you decide to go.

Here's what we'll deliver in return for your time and attention:

Actions: We've amassed tips, tools, and hints and organized them into easy-to-access chapters. We suggest you read the "Ask" and "Buck" chapters first. Then move to the others that capture your interest. And if you've read them all, have tried the ideas they suggest, and still feel you can't get what you want, reread the last chapter to ensure your next choice is the right choice.

Stories: Countless people we surveyed, worked with, talked with, or coached gave us these ideas. We heard success stories, "I messed this up" stories, and "I wish I had" stories. Find the ones that might help solve your dilemma or provoke your own creative thinking.

T-shirt truth: Ever read the message on someone's T shirt and say to yourself, "Boy, ain't that the truth?" Well, we do this all the time, and we've collected some for this book. We searched closets, memories, airports, bars, beaches, and barbeques. We narrowed it down to twenty-six that make our points.

Seen on the Riverwalk in Spokane, WA.

Think of this book as a maintenance manual for working adults seeking to tune up a significant portion of their waking lives. We invite you to return to it again and again. Dog-ear the corners; highlight the ideas that hit home. We wrote it because we truly believe you can **get more of what you want right where you are.**

***

P.S. And we'd love to hear how it turns out.
Send your stories to www.loveitdontleaveit.com.

ACKNOWLEDGMENTS

Collaboration has taught us once again the power of many minds to enrich a book. We are particularly appreciative of the wisdom from Ray Halagera; the truth telling from Diana Koch, Shelby Earl, and Tara Mello; and the savvy advice from Katherine Reynolds, Marilyn Greist, Brad Walton and Barbara Blom. We also continually tested our ideas with Ann Jordan, Bev Olevin, Sandy LoSchiavo, Lorianne Speaks, and DeeDee Williams. They helped us get on track and *stay* on track.

Nancy Breuer and Allan Halcrow (WorkPositive) helped us with brilliant editing (even our English teachers would be pleased), and Lynne Kleeger (Lynne-Worx!) was a patient perfectionist with our manuscript. Tracy Mitchell did an amazing job with our artistic needs—we greatly admire her work. Our publicists Helen Bensimon, Patti Danos, Jane Wesman, and Lori Ames have been instrumental in coaching and connecting us. Thank you!

We are indeed fortunate to have the Career Systems organization behind us every step of the way. Huge thanks go to the staff at the Scranton headquarters for their enthusiastic support and to the international sales team for helping us truly bring this book to its rightful market place. We could not translate this message into action without the experienced (and well-traveled) consultant team that partners with our clients worldwide.

The Berrett-Koehler team was (as always) encouraging, patient, straight-talking, and responsive. We published our previous books with them and did not hesitate to go directly (and only) to them for this one. They treat their authors as VIPs and supported us through the journey of creating this book.

Steve Piersanti continues to set new standards in the publishing industry and lead his organization in the most ethical and innovative style. We were touched by his faith in us and his enthusiasm for our "overachieving ways."

Bev sends appreciation to Barry and Lindsey, who brainstormed titles over the dinner table night after night and rarely lost their patience and belief that this would eventually come together. *Your support enables me to be all that I am.*

Sharon sends gratitude to her four kids—Matt, Kellie, Travis, and Shelby—for their support and enthusiasm, and especially to her husband Mike for reading every word and for providing wholehearted support. *Your creativity, work stories, and honest input helped build a book I'm proud of.*

We thank each other: Sharon to Bev for her insistence on checking with our review team "one more time"—just to be sure we're headed in the right direction; and Bev to Sharon for believing in this from the get-go and staying *on it* despite the occasional wet towel from her coauthor.

Finally, this book would never have come to fruition without all those who read *Love 'Em or Lose*

'Em and inspired us (and challenged us) to write a similar book for employees. Many read early versions of our manuscript and convinced us that we were on the right track. We want you all to find more of what you *really* want, *right where you are.*

INTRODUCTION

If it doesn't get better, I'm outta here!

***

We've all felt that way at some point in our lives. The feeling could be about work, marriage, friendships, learning a new sport, or perfecting a new skill. Or, it may not feel that extreme. You might just have a subtle sense of dissatisfaction or a mild yearning for a change. Everything could be right with your work—except for just one thing.

In the workplace, these feelings can cause you to head for the door (leave physically) or cause you to stay put but shut down (leave psychologically—turn down your energy, your *oomph.*)

> *I was present and accounted for, but not very productive. Now I realize how demoralizing it was for me, my colleagues, my friends, and even my family. Every workweek felt like a month, and my self-confidence sagged. I'll never do that again. I've learned to identify problems early and take some action to improve things. Life is too short to dread Mondays.*

Some of us give it a lot of time before we get to the point of departure (sometimes too much). Some of us give it too little time and move on too quickly.

> *I left for greener grass and found it had its own set of problems. I came back a year later.*

This place isn't perfect, but I'm more willing now to work out problems rather than leave.

Some of us take control of our own workplace satisfaction. We expect to enjoy our work, our colleagues, and our organizations and we're willing to go after those things that matter most to us.

And others just wait.

Are YOU Waiting?

Waiting for your boss to go?
Or for the economy to not be so slow?
Waiting for someone to bring fun to your work?
Or for that colleague to stop being a jerk?
Waiting for HR to chart your career?
Or for a leader to calm that downsizing fear?
Waiting for an assignment that's exciting to do?
Or for your manager to make work better for you?
Waiting for your organization to really care?
Well, guess what?
Waiting simply will not get you there!

Are you willing to stop waiting? If so, you'll get some quick, effective alternatives from the chapters ahead. We hope you'll give them a try.

What's Love Got to Do with It?

Tina Turner asked a good question. If "it" is "work," our answer is "everything." If work takes the better part of our waking lives, we'd better be in love with it or else be prepared to lead a miserable—or at minimum, boring—life. When we love our work, we unleash energy, creativity, and commitment. We look forward to the day, our teammates, the environment, the boss—the whole package. We don't want to press the snooze button. We feel productive. We feel a sense of accomplishment. We learn. *And* we feel satisfied.

The longer we stay with a job, the more we build some unique forms of equity. Consider the equity you've built in your current job:

- *Skill equity:* The knowledge, the know-how that you've developed over time. The special capabilities and competencies that bring you respect for a job well done, and enable others to count on you.
- *Social equity:* The friends and colleagues you've gotten to know (they often feel like family) or the customers you enjoy interacting with.
- *Influence equity:* The ability to get your ideas heard, the connections you've learned to use, the resources that others make available to you so you can get your job done.
- *Financial equity:* The dollars you get for the job you do. And, on top of that, the retirement, investment, or bonus funds, insurance, memberships (even perks such as a parking space), all in return for your know-how and commitment.

Looking for Love in All the Wrong Places

Sometimes we leave our workplace equity behind (too quickly) without considering how much it is, how long it will take to rebuild it, or how heavily discounted it may be somewhere else.

> *I get together with some of the old gang from where I used to work, at times just for the laughs I miss. They say that with the new leadership team, things are actually a lot better.*

***

> *I've got more freedom here, but I've got more stress, too. It's all a trade-off. Nothing is perfect.*

***

> *I got a raise and a new challenge with each of my four moves. That was great. But subsequent raises (and challenges) came very slowly and once I even went backward. Now my friends who hung in at the same place over the years are retiring with great packages. I'm wondering what I really gained.*

***

Yes, I look around every so often. But the truth is, I love having a sense of roots. This place is like a second family to me. I know the people and they know me. They've been with me through thick and thin.

All too often we depend on others to keep us from leaving, or we simply give up too quickly.

It's up to my manager to make me happy.

***

They won't give me the power to get what I want here.

***

It's easier to leave than to work it out.

***

I'm about to retire soon anyway. I'm past the point of needing to love my work.

Comments like these can contain at least a grain of truth. Managers do have a role. The lack of power does get in the way. The problems may be so huge that leaving is easier. Sometimes leaving does make sense.

But often, it doesn't.

Shift Happens

Work lives are constantly changing, just like our personal lives. Sometimes, just when you really love it, shift happens. Things change with your work, your leaders, your boss, your colleagues, your clients, your organization, the economy, the competitor, the world. And things change with you. The terrific boss moves on, the company is acquired, you get tired of the work you've been doing, or the direction of the organization shifts—right before your very eyes.

When that happens, instead of disengaging or jumping ship:

Read "Ask" and "Buck."
Then scan the table of contents
for the chapters that best fit your situation right now.

Take an idea from a story, try a checklist, or answer some of our interview questions. What's one attitude adjustment that you're willing to try? What's one small step that makes sense? Now, read another chapter.

***

You either get what you want or take what you get.

We believe you can get what you want where you are. Do you?

ASK: And You May Receive

If you don't ask, you're less likely to get what you want. It seems so simple. Yet for some reason, people hold back. They expect their bosses to read their minds. Some just settle for less and bring half their hearts (or brains) to work. Others decide it's easier to leave than to ask. Most people eventually realize that no matter where or with whom they work, at times they will want a little more of something. And the best way to get that something is to ask.

What you don't ask for stays the same.

—Unknown

They Want to Hear from You

If you are a solid performer, your managers want to know what will keep you engaged (satisfied, productive) and on the team. They don't want to lose you, physically or psychologically.

I wish he had just asked. I would have said, "Let me see what I can do for you. Let's brainstorm how this might work—for you and for others." Instead of asking, he jumped ship. I am so disappointed. We needed him. He had a great future here.

How ready are you to hold an honest, possibly courageous conversation with your boss, a colleague, a senior leader? How willing are you to ask for what you really want? Here's how someone did just that:

I considered quitting my job rather than asking for time off to participate in an overseas service/study program. It just seemed like too big a request. I thought the answer would be no, especially since our department has been so stretched and stressed lately. But I love this job, and my boss is great. I didn't want to leave. I got some coaching from a friend, created a plan, and just went for it.

I told my boss I was a little nervous about a request I had. But I explained the opportunity in detail, told him what I thought I would gain from it and also what I believed he and my team might gain. For example, I believed I would return with new leadership skills and a more global perspective. In our line of work, both could be valuable assets.

I described seven barriers or downsides of my sabbatical and asked him to add to the list. Then I shared some potential solutions to many of those barriers. An example was finding and training an intern to cover much of my work load while I was gone. I also promised to brainstorm solutions to every other barrier with him and my team.

When I was done, he simply said, "Yes." I sat there in shock. He told me he was impressed with my thoughtful approach and my courage (he knew how nervous I was). I thanked him that day, and many times since. We worked on the details over the next two months. I took my trip and came back to work refreshed, energized, and more capable.

My boss and I are both glad that I asked, rather than leave that job. The way I thank him now is by doing my best at work.

Who do you need to ask? And for what? How will you go about it? Try the following steps.

Step 1: Get Crystal-Clear about What You Want

I had this gnawing feeling of dissatisfaction. I would have talked to someone about what I wanted, but first I had to put my finger on it. I'm clear now. I want to feel recognized for what I do here—and I don't mean more money (although that would be nice). I want my boss to say "Thank you" more often. Not just thanks in general but specifically thanks after I've worked late or done a great job on a project. I need to know she values me and my work.

So, what do you want? Get to the bottom of it. Interview yourself:

- What about my job makes me jump out of bed in the morning?
- What makes me hit the snooze button?
- If I were to win the lottery and resign, what would I miss the most?
- What would be the one change in my current role that would make me want to stay for a *long* time?
- If I had a magic wand, what would be the one thing I would change about my department or team?
- If I had to go back to a position in my past and stay for an extended period of time, which one would it be and why?

The answers to these questions will reveal what you want. Other chapters in this book will help you further clarify your "wish list." **Reread "Ask" after reading them.**

Step 2: Consider Who, When, and How You'll Ask

Who can deliver what you want? Consider these people:

- Those with information you need
- Good listeners and advice givers
- Decision makers (your boss?)

How and when will you approach them? Consider their preferences:

- Should you request the conversation by e-mail, voice mail, or face-to-face?
- Is it best to meet early in the morning or over lunch? Monday or later in the week?

How will you open the conversation? Consider these guidelines:

- Get to the point. Thank the person for his or her time and say you have a request to make.
- Lay it out and be specific. What do you need? Advice? Feedback? A new challenge?

Step 3: Identify the Barriers—Then Bulldoze Them

Barriers to asking come in all shapes and sizes. Here are some of the most common:

- **Fear.** Is *fear* in the way of asking? Fear of what? The answer? The person? Something else?

  I remembered reading somewhere that I should 'face the fear and do it anyway.' I think the author meant if it's not life threatening. So, after a few sleepless nights and several rounds of practice with my friend, I just went for it. It wasn't nearly as frightening as I thought it would be. I got out of there with my life, and I'm optimistic about getting what I want.

It's simple. To get more of what you really want at work, face your fear, plan your approach, and go for it.

Courage is resistance to fear, mastery of fear, not absence of fear.

—Mark Twain

- **Your boss's (or other decision makers') mind-sets, constraints, or concerns.** Those you ask are often bound by rules, policies, guidelines, and cultural norms. And they're concerned about fairness.

  I knew he'd be worried about my teammates and their re actions if he said yes to my request. I listed three ways I thought we could handle that concern. He came up with another. Together we dealt with the team in such a positive way that they were actually happy for me. They are also happy to have a boss whom they know will listen to them when they want something!

  Anticipate the problems and potential barriers to your request and present ideas for solving them. Seek solutions that work for you, them, and the team.
- **Lack of WIIFT (what's in it for them?).** Before you go to your request granter, stop and identify the WIIFT. Ask yourself, "What's in it for that person to grant my request? How will she benefit? Is

my request a 'piece of cake' or really difficult to grant?" WIIFT in hand, now you're ready to ask.

I wanted to learn from her. I knew it was probably the last thing she'd want to do, meet with another grad student. She was so busy and rarely in the office. So, I offered three hours of research time in exchange for one hour of he rtime with me. She paused a minute and then said, "Yes, what a great idea."

Find the WIIFT and you'll increase the odds of getting a yes.

And If the Answer Is No?

Despite your careful planning and strategic thinking, you'll no doubt encounter a no now and then. Listen to the reasons for the no. Then:

ask again (in a different way or at a different time)

—or—

ask how *you* can help make it work (brainstorm possibilities)

—or—

ask someone else (can someone else help with your request?)

—or—

ask what's possible, if not this

—or—

ask when it might be possible, if not now

—or—

Seen at the Rose Bowl Flea Market in Pasadena, CA.

ask what you can do to improve the way you're asking.

Don't give up.

The best advice I ever got was from a salesman. He said every no he received got him closer to the inevitable yes.

And when they say yes, *thank them*—with words and in continued great performance.

***

People tell us that in hindsight, they wish they had asked for what they wanted. Or they wish they'd asked in a more effective way, so a decision maker could have worked with them to make it happen. Asking is key to every chapter and central to the philosophy of this book.

Don't expect others to take the first step. Don't make them guess, because most often, they'll

guess wrong. Be clear. Be prepared. Be collaborative, and then *ask for what you want.*

If you don't ask for what you want, you'll simply have to take what you get.

BUCK: Don't Pass It

Some people are tempted to hold others accountable for their work satisfaction. Most find over time that those others can't—or won't—deliver what's wanted and needed. Ultimately you choose your career, your boss, your team, your organization. You decide how long to stay, and you have the power and influence to improve your work. Accept that responsibility, complete with its challenges, and you'll get more of what you want from your work and your workplace.

If It's to Be, It's Up to Me

You may have heard that quote before. And you may even have found it annoying. Annoying, but true.

> *I pushed the snooze button again. It was Monday morning, and the last thing I wanted to do was get up and go to work. I drank another cup of coffee, dropped off the dry cleaning, and actually felt relieved about the traffic jam that delayed my arrival even more.*
>
> *After months of feeling this way, I decided no one was going to do a thing about it—but me.*

My boss isn't the type to have a conversation with me about my career, and no one was offering me an exciting new opportunity.

One night I took my wife to dinner and told her I had to do something about my work. I had to leave or make it better. We spent the next three hours writing down all of my options and talking about several strategies.

I started researching some of those options the following week. I talked with my boss about doing more of the work I love and less of the work I dislike. I also talked about options with several colleagues and even a manager in another department. In all of that exploration, I found a colleague who actually loves to do what I hate! With my boss's help, we've redesigned both my colleague's job and mine. I still work in the same company, even for the same boss, but my day-to-day work has changed by 80 percent.

Get this. On a Sunday night, I actually felt excited about the workweek ahead. What a relief!

How have you taken charge lately?

- I've carefully evaluated and listed (in detail) what I love about work and what I don't. (yes/no)
- I've looked at my latest performance review and identified a step I could take to improve. (yes/no)
- I've chatted with a sympathetic (smart) partner about work and what I want from it. (yes/no)
- I've clearly evaluated my role in a workplace dilemma or dissatisfaction. (yes/no)

- I've explored and then listed *all* of my options. (yes/no)
- I've identified what is possible and what isn't, given this organization's culture, leadership, or rules. (yes/no)
- I've taken a risk and
  talked to people who might be able to help me (yes/no)
  —or—
  tried something new. (yes/no)

If you answered no to any of these, it's simple: *Do it.*

Even if you're on the right track, you'll get run over if you just sit there.

—Will Rogers

Beware the Blame Game

Seen at a Grateful Dead concert, late 1960s.

When you point a finger, remember that three other fingers are pointing back at you.

It's so easy to blame. For most of us, the excuses and finger pointing are a knee-jerk reaction. It's a normal, human defense. But blaming seldom gets us what we really want and need.

> *It's called the Blame Game. You know, when you point the finger and say, "He did it. She did it. They did it." I was into that game big-time until a friend suggested I stop whining and take some accountability for my unhappy work situation. (Yes, friends will tell you the truth!) I realized that I was bored and had basically retired on the job. It wasn't all my fault, but it wasn't really all theirs, either. I talked to my boss about doing something new. He had no idea how bored I was and has helped me find new, more challenging work. I'm learning again and happy with my job.*

***

This entire book is about taking responsibility for your own satisfaction. The "Buck" philosophy supports the messages in all other chapters. If you don't buy "B," you'll never get to "Z."

Yes, others have roles to play in your work success and happiness. But none have roles that equal yours. Ultimately, it's up to you to change what you don't like and to find what you really want at work.

CAREER: Chart Your Course

Your career is your creation. So when was the last time you really gave serious thought and time to planning it? If you can't remember, is it because:

- You are too busy doing this job to think about the next?
- You don't know what you want to do next?
- You are waiting for your manager to make the first move?
- You think the future is too uncertain for career planning?

Too many people allow one or more of these thoughts to delay or even paralyze their actions. They wait. For certainty. For their bosses to provide career maps. For a revelation about the next step. For a "time-out" from the current work, to ponder the next. The truth is that only you can make the time and the decisions that put your career on the right course. The payoff? Greater work satisfaction.

> *I had done a great job here for twelve years. I knew that I'd be promoted eventually. I waited for the promotion and when it didn't come, I finally asked my boss about it. He said, "Sorry, but in addition to your work experience, that job now*

requires a special technical certificate." I had watched some colleagues taking those classes, but just didn't realize it was such a big deal. This past year I took the classes and earned the certificate. Recently I finally got that promotion. Now I've gone "public" with my career goals. I talk about them with my boss and am constantly looking for ways to attain them.

Whose Career Is It, Anyway?

You *own* your career. This attitude will help you get what you want from work. Take steps now to plan it, build it, and strengthen it. Here's how:

- *Look at yourself*—Examine your interests, values, and work skills. Find out, too, if others see you the way you see yourself.
- *Look around*—Uncover trends (company/industry), learning pathways (ways to learn new skills), and multiple career options.
- *Look ahead*—Identify goals, alliances, support. Create your plan.

Talk with colleagues, friends, and bosses. Identify and collaborate with people interested in helping you. Think about how you, in turn, can help them. Use them as sounding boards to test your ideas, career options, and assumptions.

Here's Lookin' at You

Assess. It's the critical first step in successfully managing your career.

Know Yourself

What do you love to do? To create a meaningful career pathway, you need to be clear about your interests (the things you like doing—ideas and activities that give fulfillment and pleasure) and your values (ideals you cherish that guide your life at work). Determine those critical variables. **Interview yourself:**

- What accomplishments at work have made me feel particularly proud?
- What makes me feel unique in this organization?
- What kinds of things would I do if I could create my ideal workday?
- What types of work do I avoid?

The things you do well, value highly, and like doing give you a basic map for planning your career. Look for opportunities to do that *inside* your organization.

Know Your Strengths

What are your key skills (effective abilities and/or behaviors used to produce clear results)?

How do you know? **Interview yourself and three others (teammates, boss, friends):**

- What are my towering strengths? (Very few people are as good as I am.)
- What are my moderate strengths? (I'm good—so are many others.)
- How would customers (internal or external) describe me?

Are you using your key skills? Most people we know are not unhappy because of the skills they are using—but because of the skills they are not using.

> ***Know which of your skills is irrepressible!***
>
> —Dick Bolles, author of *What Color Is Your Parachute?*

Know What You Need to Learn

Given your interests, what do you need/want to learn? Ask yourself. Also, gather information from three willing feedback providers:

- What are my overdone strengths? (too much of a good thing)

  I am bottom-line oriented. I get results. The problem is that in getting there, I sometimes run over people.
- What are two skills I should strengthen? How would it help me, given what I want to do?

My career goal is to move up in this organization. Two of my strengths are that I'm detail oriented and very independent. I've always figured I had to do it myself if I wanted it done right. Now I'm hearing that I need to learn to "manage through others"—not do it myself—if I hope to move into management positions. I need to develop some new strengths.

Seek out your critics. Listen to them. Try to see yourself through their eyes. Get clear about your missing skills or those skills you overdo.

Lookin' Around

Once you've assessed what you need to learn, you can begin to look around your organization for trends, learning pathways, and career options. You may be surprised to find projects, task forces, and jobs that will support your goals.

Trend Tracking

What do you know about your organization, your industry, and your profession? If you don't know the answers to these questions, ask others:

- What are the major industry, economic, political, and social changes taking place that will affect this organization?
- What are the opportunities and problems ahead?
- How will my profession be different in two years? In five years?

- What counts for success here? How will that change in the future?

Read company newsletters and industry journals. Search for Web sites that discuss your industry. Bookmark them and check them regularly.

Learning Pathways: The 70-20-10 Rule

How do adults learn? One well-known answer (described by the Center for Creative Leadership in Greensboro, North Carolina) suggests the following:

- 70 percent of adult learning happens by doing. On-the-job challenges, risky situations, and stretch assignments all contribute to success at work.
- 20 percent of adult learning comes from others. Mentors, role models, feedback providers, and coaches help us develop and excel.
- 10 percent of adult learning happens in the classroom, from books, tapes, or on-line learning activities.

So, choose a learning pathway that works for you and will best develop the skill you're trying to learn. Try this:

- Offer to serve on a project team or task force that will help you develop a skill or make key connections.
- Agree to a tough assignment. Be sure to ask for support from those who've been there and/or done that.

- Find a mentor to teach you the specific skill you're hoping to learn.
- Take a class (ask about education reimbursement options), or read a couple of books on the topic of interest.

Ask yourself, "What do I want to learn next? How/where/from whom can I learn it?"

Options, Options, Options

Not every step in a career has to be a step up. *Up* is one way to go, but there are other options (inside the organization) to consider, too. Talk to your boss or other valued advisors to learn about these possibilities:

- *Moving laterally*—a change in job, but not necessarily a change in level of responsibility
- *Exploring*—testing and researching changes without permanent commitment
- *Enriching*—seeding the current job with more chances to learn and grow
- *Realigning*—adjusting duties to reconcile them with other priorities and future possibilities

Try to imagine at least one move you could make in each of these directions. What would it look like? How might it match your skills, interests, and values?

Now, Create the Plan

Use the information you now have about you, your company, and multiple options to develop your career

Seen in a Jacksonville, FL bookstore.

goals. Those goals will become the cornerstone of an action plan, so take care to make them specific and achievable.

Answer these questions:

- What new skills, knowledge, or abilities do I need to achieve my goals?
- What are some short-term goals (three to six months) that I could start on right now?
- How can I gain the new skills that will help me with my goals while in my *current* job?
- What relevant experiences can I have through serving on committees and task forces?
- Who in my network can help?

A clear plan of action turns goals into realities if you take these steps:

- Write down your goals, exact steps, and deadlines. Revise along the way.
- Forge alliances with people who can help you reach your goals: managers, mentors, peers, supporters.

- Seek learning. Get training and experience to help you reach your goals.

  I read a book about career planning and decided to fill in the blanks and develop a plan, including specific action steps. Six months later, I had not taken a single action! It was like my New Year's resolution—so easy to disregard. Finally, a friend in another department told me some of her career goals, and I unearthed my action plan to show her. Right away she pointed out items that were simply unrealistic or didn't sound like me. With her feedback, I adjusted my plan and sought another approach that made more sense.

***

Charting your course can feel like an overwhelming task, somewhere between keeping New Year's resolutions and raising the Titanic. Yet, it's doable if you look at yourself, look around, and look ahead. What you learn goes into your plan. Obviously you'll need allies, relevant projects, and an organization that values what you do. But you're in charge of your career. You manage it within your company, within this economy, and with the capabilities and resources that you have.

If you fail to plan, you are planning to fail.

—Anonymous

DIGNITY: Give It to Get it

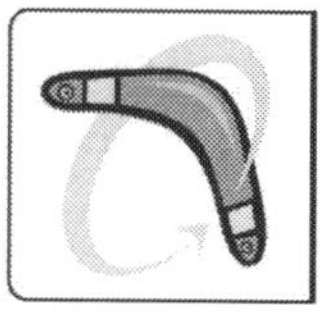

Aretha Franklin sang it—

> **"R.E.S.P.E.C.T—find out what it means to me."**

Aretha made a lot of sense (and cents, too) with her hit refrain. Respect has different meanings to different people. To receive it, you have to spell out what respect means to you.

The respect you get influences how much you love (or don't love) your work. Many dissatisfied people dislike their jobs because they don't feel respected—for who they are or what they do. If you don't feel respected, don't just wait and hope for your boss, colleagues, or employees to give it to you. Clarify what respect means to you. Tell someone what you want and need in order to feel more respected. Find ways to get more respect, right where you are.

> *When I was promoted to a project lead role, I was told I needed to be more "leaderlike." What on Earth did that mean? I asked several people that question, including my boss. She said that I*

was respected as a researcher, but not as a leader in the organization. She said (and others agreed) that I should speak up in meetings, that I was just too quiet and people assumed I had nothing of value to contribute—otherwise, I would have talked more.

I was shocked and hurt at first. I never want to pretend to be someone I'm not, and frankly I don't respect some of the "conversation hogs" on the team.

I decided to go after the respect that was missing. I found a colleague who encouraged me to try some new behaviors, including offering my suggestions and ideas in meetings. She suggested I find a new way to participate, like adding my opinion from time to time, while still being myself. After months of my trying new and subtle changes, people started noticing and told me how much they valued my input.

I let go of some of my own biases and changed some of my behaviors to get the respect I wanted. In the process I found ways to respect my outspoken colleagues for what they bring to the party. We're different—but that difference actually makes our team stronger.

This researcher looked for the "grain of truth" in the feedback she got from others, and she *chose* to make some changes. In the process, she learned to value the style diversity on her team.

To "get more respect," try this:

First and foremost, make sure you're a solid performer (meeting your goals consistently). Solid performers almost always get more respect.

Then:

- Figure out who *does* and *doesn't* respect you and why. Ask a friend at work to tell you honestly how much you're respected and why. Listen for what's true in the feedback. Listen for the good news, too. Sometimes we're so focused on negative feedback, we forget to notice and celebrate the positive.
- Tell someone that you want and need more respect. Ideally, tell the one who can *give* you what you want. Be specific about what it would look like. Say, "I'd feel more respected if you did more of this or less of this." Many people think they're respectful but are missing the mark. They might appreciate your frank input and your clear request to do something differently.

My teammate was shocked when I told her I didn't really feel respected by her. She said she does respect me and then listed several reasons why. She thought she already was respectful but agreed to try supporting my ideas in a new, more visible way. Specifically, she'll speak up on my behalf in meetings with my boss and teammates. That's exactly what I want and need from her.

- Decide on the changes you *want* to make to get more respect. Decide on changes you *don't want* to make.

And—Give It to Get It!

With respect, what goes around comes around.

Check out your own respect-giving tendencies. Do you respect others? How? When?

I went with my family to the Museum of Tolerance in Los Angeles. What an experience. I entered knowing that I don't have a prejudiced bone in my body, and I left realizing I do have a few leanings. Those leanings affect my dealings with colleagues, bosses, even customers. I'm working on them, and some of my attitudes are slowly shifting—for the better.

Leanings Check

Be honest. Admit to your leanings toward or away from those with different

- skin color,
- status,
- personality,
- age,
- education,
- height or weight,
- title,
- accent,

- geographic origin,
- job function,
- gender,
- lifestyle,
- sexual orientation,
- talent,
- _____ (add one), and
- _____ (add another).

How do your leanings affect your ability to feel and demonstrate respect for others? Do you talk to some more or involve some less? If you see a *leaning* getting in your way, decide to change. It may take a little time because *old leanings die hard.* Stick with it. As you respect others, you'll feel respect come flowing back to you.

GREETINGS. I am pleased to see that we are different. May we together become greater than the sum of both of us.

—Mr. Spock of *Star Trek*

***

You deserve respect. We all do. Get your share by performing well, by asking for it, by continually improving, and yes, by being willing to change *YOU* in small but significant ways.

Seen in a church parking lot in Woodinville, WA.

ENRICH: Energize Your Work

I've lost the energy and enthusiasm for my work. There's nothing really wrong, except the challenge and excitement seem to be gone. I wonder if it's time to move on.

Maybe it's not time to move on. Maybe it's time to look at how to breathe life back into your work—how to give it some CPR (Career Path Resuscitation).

There's a good chance that you can enhance and energize your work, right where you are. And, if you like *most* aspects of the work (the people, your boss, the tasks you perform), it's definitely worth a try. Enrichment means finding a way to get the growth, challenge, or renewal you seek without leaving your current job. Changing what you do (content) or how you do it (process) is the key.

Don't resign yourself to "ho-hum" work. And don't wait for your boss or someone else in the organization to put the spark back in your work. They may not even know you've *lost* it. Or they may not know what to do about it. Take charge and do something *now* to energize your work.

Job Judo—Go with the Energy

In judo, you use the momentum of the other person to increase your own energy and effectiveness. You build on the energy coming your way. Similarly, in *job* judo, the key is to build on the energy that comes from doing what you love. First, determine what really gives you energy. Is it:

- using your current skills in new settings?
- learning new skills and applying them?
- having greater visibility, challenge, or reward?
- getting to do more things that reflect your values?
- something else?

Pay attention to your energy level. Be aware of when it wanes and when it surges. Think about what causes the difference.

> *I had zero interest in another round of construction project scheduling and budgeting. But then I saw a demonstration of a sophisticated computer program that schedules and budgets for you if you just plug in numbers. Intrigued, I shared my excitement with my boss and explained that it would free me up for more important tasks. He agreed to send me to training. Now I spend half my time troubleshooting on-site, instead of working with the numbers. This is far more interesting—I'm excited again.*

Energy Matching

Think about what energizes you. Then find a place to invest that energy. Some examples appear in the following chart.

Try job judo. You might be surprised at the enrichment opportunities you can find, right in your own backyard.

If You're Energized by:	
Independence	Projects/tasks you can manage with little supervision.
Feedback	Peers, internal customers, or a boss willing to give you the straight story about something specific.
Challenge	A chance to do something that will really stretch you (speaking to senior leaders, chairing a task force, doing work in a new area).
Customer contact	Ways to interface more with internal or external customers. Take them to lunch, troubleshoot with them, and attend their conferences.
Teamwork	A group that is solving a work problem or form a team. Consider a sports team as well.
Learning	Someone who will teach you something new. Consider a class outside of work, surf the Internet, or read a book.
Variety	A way to vary your work schedule, place of work, or the tasks you perform day to day. Even reconsider the route you take to work.
Leadership	Someone who needs and wants mentoring or coaching. Consider opportunities inside or outside work.

If You're Energized by:	
Decision making	A way to have input about work processes before they are cast in stone. Volunteer to be on a decision-making committee. Join a community organization—take your pick.

I thrive on variety—in life and at work. If I've been doing the same thing in the same way for six months, I'm ready for a change. Instead of leaving the organization this time, I decided to talk with my boss about ways to spice up my work. He has supported me in job rotation with several people on the team. We all feel challenged and interested as we learn new things. And we can serve as backup for each other any time that it's needed. Everyone wins.

Learning Assignments—Give Yourself One

Think back to a time when you felt the most energized about your work. What were you doing? Among other things, most people would say they were *learning.* Is that true for you? If so, you might enrich your work by giving yourself a learning assignment.

Identify a skill (or trait) that is not your strength and one that you *want to learn* (a "development" opportunity). Now, create an on-the-job learning assignment for the purpose of developing that new skill (or trait). Here's an example:

You want to become a better negotiator. Your learning assignment could include steps toward developing the new skill:

1. *Conscious observation:* Find an expert negotiator you could observe. Then find another (for comparison). Take notes as you observe. What did they do well? How were they similar or different in their negotiating style? Chat with both negotiators after the observation period. Discuss what worked best and why. What would they do differently next time? (If you can't find someone to observe, watch a great video on negotiating.)
2. *Selected participation:* Take a well-defined, limited role in a negotiation. Partner with an expert who will let you try out the new skill but is there to help when you stumble. The goal is to get your feet wet without feeling overwhelmed. You could, for example, prepare the opening remarks in a negotiation with a vendor, then watch your partner work her magic. When it's over, ask for specific feedback about your strengths and weaknesses.
3. *Key responsibility:* After completing steps one and two, take primary responsibility for a negotiation. You might "up the ante" by choosing one that is highly visible. For example, you might lead the negotiation with a vendor in

front of your team. Assign skilled negotiators as observers. They will take notes as *you* work your magic. Meet with them immediately after the negotiation to get feedback.

After this three-step process, you'll be amazed at your growing expertise in the new skill or trait. Keep practicing as you strive for excellence. And notice how energized you feel throughout this process.

Bite off more than you can chew, then chew it.

—Ella Williams

REMEMBER: You can also stretch and enrich your work by:

- using your existing skills in new ways and settings;
- using some skills more and others less;
- refreshing skills you haven't had a chance to use in a while.

Sell It Up

If you have an enrichment idea you truly want to try, you may need to sell it to your manager. Prepare yourself by answering the following questions:

What's in it for me?

- How will it increase my marketability in my profession?

- How will it increase my reputation as a specialist or generalist?
- How will it help me gain more confidence and competence?

What's in it for my work group?

- How will it help me work more effectively with my current team?
- How will it increase/enhance my contribution to my group or department?
- How does it build new relationships or extend my network?

What's in it for my boss or the organization?

- How will it increase my value to the boss or organization?
- How does it contribute to current organizational mission, strategy, or goals?
- How does it address a current relevant business need?

It's hard for a boss to resist a request for enrichment, especially one that is well thought out and beneficial to your work group, organization, or your own satisfaction and commitment.

***

You might think you have to move to another position or another organization to feel energized about your work again. You don't. In today's work environment there is almost always something new to learn, another

approach to try, or a way to rekindle enthusiasm. Don't wait for someone to hand you an exciting project or something new to learn. Find a way to enrich your *own* work, negotiate for it, and then do it.

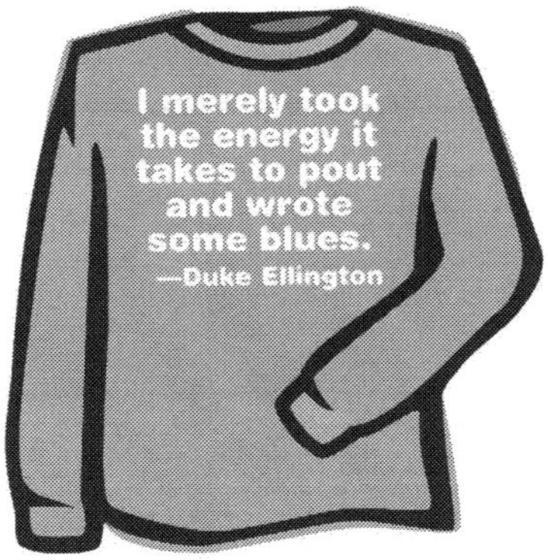

Seen on James Street, Scranton, PA.

FAMILY: Seen Yours Lately?

How's your family? Is anyone complaining about not seeing enough of you? If you're waiting for your boss (or the work/life task force) to recognize and address your need for work/life balance, forget it. It's up to you to decide what you want and to go after it yourself.

And, by the way, the definition of *family* has broadened. When we asked people who their family is, we heard:

- "My wife (husband/partner) and our kids."
- "My friends at work."
- "My aging mom (dad)."
- "My weekend buddies."
- "My dog (cat, bird, iguana)."

Our definitions of *family* may differ, but their importance to us is crystal clear. We want and deserve time with them.

> *I got the hint loud and clear when my five-year-old made a paperclip "chain" and strung it across the door to my home office. I was locked out.*

Is anyone in your life trying to give you a hint?

Get Creativeing

You may think you're trapped. You might believe there is no way to excel at work and have quality time with your family. But we've seen dozens of people *effectively* integrate career and family. Here are some of the creative strategies we've heard about. Think about which might work for you:

> *My boss agreed that a colleague and I could try job sharing (each working half-time). That was ten years ago, and it has worked great. What a win-win for all of us!*

***

> *I took a time management course and have carved four hours out of my workweek. I'm now working smarter, not longer, and I have more time away from work.*

***

> *I have a home office. I didn't know how to break the routine of going there every night. Someone gave me the easiest suggestion. Just don't go down there on Saturday nights. That I could do. Soon I was out of the habit, and then I extended it to Sunday nights as well. It was a small step but made a big difference.*

***

I bought a home computer and then approached my boss to consider my telecommuting one day a week. He said it was okay, as long as my productivity didn't drop. It actually went up 20 percent. My boss is thrilled, and so is my family.

***

My dog is my family. She's well behaved, so my boss agreed that I could bring her to work on Saturdays when I came in to "catch up." She's not alone, and neither am I.

***

I travel a lot and hate being away from my family. Last year I decided to take them with me on three trips. We found hotels with swimming pools and enjoyed the adventure together.

***

I shifted my hours. I now go into work at 6:30A.M. and miss most of the rush hour traffic, going both ways. That way I can be home early for dinner with my family.

***

I found daycare close to the office. I walk there and have lunch with my kids at least three days a week. I'm getting exercise, a break from work, and quality time with my family.

What good is a high-powered career if it makes you miserable?

What good is owning a beautiful house if you're never home?

What good is being passionate about a hobby if you never have the free time to pursue it?

—Pamela Kruger, *Fast Company* magazine

Try something innovative or nontraditional. Creativity will help you solve the balance issue.

Get Inclusive

You might better balance family and work if you merge them more. Think about how you might involve your family in your work world. These people did that. Try something similar:

My company held a "bring-your-family-to-work" day. I did that and couldn't believe the difference it made. My kids were fascinated by the airplanes I had helped build. They seemed so proud and are much more tolerant of my "late-to-dinner" evenings. I plan to take them to the next company picnic, too.

***

I was a single mom, balancing work, young kids, and graduate school. We instituted study hours, where we spread our work all over the kitchen countertop and spent an hour every night and several on the weekend focused on work or school. Then we watched a favorite TV show or went for pizza or a movie. We still remember fondly that time spent together.

***

My husband is involved in my creative endeavors, in a very important way. He brainstorms with me, shares stories from his workplace, and gives me critical feedback. I think his involvement helps him understand the pressures (and joys) of my work. I benefit from his insight and perspective.

***

My friends are family to me. They showed up to help me move from one workplace to another. I showed them around the office and explained the work we do there. It was great to share that part of my life with them. Amid the boxes and chaos of moving, we had a great day.

You can include your family in your work in ways you'll all enjoy. That merging of two important aspects of your life will bring a new sense of well-being and balance.

Get Focused

At work you're thinking about family. At home, you're thinking about work. Think of the wasted, guilt-ridden hours spent in both situations. These people found ways to get focused (at home *and* at work) and have more quality time with family:

I've unleashed myself on the weekend—no beeper or cell phone. I explained to my boss that I need to unplug now and then. He seemed to understand, and in fact, I think he's trying to do the same. Now weekends belong to the family.

***

My office is at home. The good news is I can sneak in any time and do some work. The bad news is it's right there and hard to ignore. I established official office hours. I now turn the phone ringer off and close the office door at 5:30P.M.

***

When I'm with my family and my mind starts to wander toward work, I force myself to picture a red stop sign. Then I bring myself back to the present and to them.

***

I wasn't focusing enough at work. I got distracted easily and wasn't delegating effectively, either. As a result my work days were getting longer and my time with family shorter. I overhauled my typical work day. Now I close my office door for an hour every morning so that I can focus, uninterrupted, on key tasks. I also delegate more effectively. I'm more productive at work, and I get home earlier these days. It's all about focusing.

Increase your focus on work when you're there by making that focus a priority for the next few weeks. Then do the same with your family. You'll notice your success and satisfaction goes up.

Most people are so busy knocking themselves out trying to do everything they think they should do, they never get around to what they want to do.

—Kathleen Windsor, author

***

If you do nothing but complain, you do nothing to fix your situation. Go to your boss and others with solid information and creative suggestions. You shouldn't have to choose between work and family. You can have both. Get *creative,* get *inclusive,* and get *focused.*

Seen in a New York City deli.

GOALS: Up Is Not the Only Way

The only career path I saw was up—and up was in short supply.

—Hundreds of workers we've known

What if the promotion you want is not available? What if the corporate ladder has lost a few rungs? How else might you move (and grow) inside this organization, if not up?

And who will determine what the "next steps" are for you? If you're waiting for your boss (or someone else) to define and then deliver your career path, you might wait a *long* time. In this rapidly changing work world, *the path* becomes a moving target. The department or job you covet today could be gone tomorrow. And besides, you're in charge of your own career. No one will ever care as much about your future as you do.

So, consider multiple career options and investigate them thoroughly. In so doing, you'll get more of what you really want. As you look at the following options, ask, "Which might give you more choice and leverage? How many can you pursue at the same time?"

Goals are dreams with deadlines.

—Diana Scharf Hunt

The Lateral Option (Moving Across or Horizontally)

I hope to move into a senior leadership role here someday. To prepare me for that eventual step, they've moved me out of Operations and into Sales. What a shock it's been. Everything is different here—the culture, the way work gets done, the interface with customers. I'm out of my comfort zone—but I'm definitely learning.

It used to be the kiss of death. "Did you hear? He's taking a *lateral!*" Lateral moves meant that a person was being sidelined, benched, or bypassed.

Today many upwardly focused individuals realize that lateral moves provide much-needed experience. Others take a lateral move because the work interests them more or they just want a change. Taking a lateral move gives you a chance to apply your skills in a new job at the same level, but with different duties or challenges. Lateral moves can improve and expand your skills or perhaps shift them from a slow-growing part of the organization to one that is growing faster.

To see if a lateral move could work for you, **interview yourself:**

- What do I need to learn?
- Which of my skills can I use beyond my present job and present department?
- If I take a lateral move, how can that job bring me closer to my goal?
- What other department interests me?

The Enrichment Option (Growing in Place)

> *I worked as a project manager for a great boss, but I knew that I could do more. I have fantastic artistic skills (if I do say so myself), and my boss knew about them. I did a few great "volunteer" projects for her that demonstrated my skill. She sent me to a desktop publishing class, and now I use my new skills constantly. I am thrilled!*

Most folks seem to think they need to move out of their current position to develop. Never has this been less true. You can enrich your current work by expanding the job, refining your expertise, or finding depth in areas you really enjoy.

To see if enrichment is what you want, **interview yourself:**

- What do I enjoy most about my job? How might I do more of it?
- What could be added to my job to make it more satisfying? More energizing?
- Which of my current tasks is the most routine? Could I do less of it? (Could I switch certain responsibilities with a coworker?)

The Exploratory Option (Temporary Move to Research Other Options)

> *I worked in information technology (IT), and the best part of my job was teaching others. I wondered if I might prefer working in the Training Department. I asked my boss if there was a way I could explore that possibility. He worked with the training manager and agreed to "loan" me for ten weeks. Now I'm back in IT and think I want to stay here, as long as I get to do a lot of teaching. I'm glad I got to check out another option here, though.*

It happens. Sometimes we aren't sure of what we want, what choices are available, or even what's appropriate. We need information to decide if the grass is indeed greener elsewhere.

To see if exploration makes sense, **interview yourself:**

- What other areas of the company interest me? How can I learn more about them?

- If I could start my career over, what would I do differently? Is that still possible? What could I do in my current position to pursue that option?
- Which task forces or project teams interest me?
- Which assignment might give me the best view of another part of this organization?
- Whose job would I like to learn more about? How and when can I meet with the person in that job?

The Realignment Option (Moving Downward)

You might think, "That's worse than a *lateral!*" But consider:

> *I was a nursing supervisor for ten years. One day I woke up and said, "I don't really like managing people. Why am I doing this job?" I took a step down in some people's eyes, but for me it was a huge improvement. I left management and went back to taking care of people—which is why I became a nurse in the first place. I love my job and will continue doing it as long as I'm able.*

***

> *I finally reached my goal. I became an IT manager. It only took me six months to realize I loved to code. I code very well and I missed it ... a lot. I was smart enough to do something*

about it—but it took guts to step out of management.

Reaching your ultimate goals—better work, more balance in life, more fun, more money—sometimes requires an apparent step backward.

To see if realignment might make sense, **interview yourself:**

- If I take a step down into another area, what would the benefits be? Would I gain more (learning, balance, health, fun)?
- Am I willing to accept the same or a lower salary to try a different job? What other "benefits" might I lose (flexibility, input, decision making, etc.)?
- How could a step down help me to use the skills I really enjoy? What things do I enjoy now that I would no longer get to do?
- Do I miss the technical, hands-on work I used to do?

One of the greatest joys in life is to be in search of one thing and to discover another.

—Anne Wilson Schaef

The Vertical Option (Moving to the Next Rung on the Career Ladder)

Vertical advancement, or moving up the corporate ladder, is the classic career goal. What would a vertical option look like for you? Of course, advancement is most likely to happen when your abilities match the organization's needs. If this is your goal, you must interpret the organization's strategic direction and carefully consider how you could prepare for this step.

> *I went to my boss and told him that I wanted his job, someday. He chuckled and said he wasn't planning to go anywhere soon, but he'd help me with my goal of moving up. We talked about my career often as I learned and grew and prepared myself for promotion. Finally, it came and I was prepared. He moved on and I interviewed for his job. My skills perfectly matched the organization's strategic goals and direction. I was selected for the job of my dreams. It took time and patience and effort on my part—but I reached my goal. Time to set the next one.*

To see if vertical makes sense, **interview yourself:**

- Who is my competition for that next position? What are my strengths and weaknesses relative to the other person?
- How have I performed during the last year? In what ways do I need to improve? Have I consistently taken on added responsibilities?
- Why should this company promote me? What value do I bring?
- What are the satisfactions and headaches that might come with this vertical move?

Your goal should be out of reach, not out of sight.

—Anita DeFrantz

The Relocation Option (Moving On)

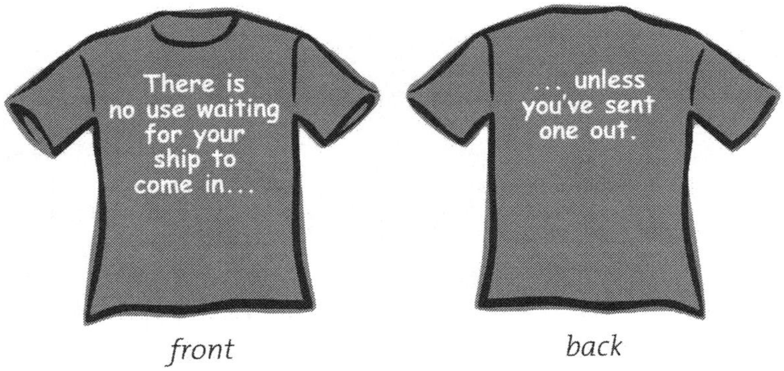

Seen at Ghiradelli Square, San Francisco, CA.

My business unit has changed direction suddenly. The work I loved doing would become a small, insignificant part of the organization's strategic direction. I had to go.

You have researched all options and you believe you need to leave. Why? Which of these are true for you?

- Your skills, interests, and values just don't fit your work.
- Your career goals are unrealistic for your organization.
- Your technical skills are no longer needed in your organization.

- Your personal life goals (you want to live in Maui) don't mesh with this work (it's in Antarctica).

If you think the only way to reach your goals is to go, **interview yourself:**

- Do I know other people who have left this company and gone somewhere else? What did they think six months later?
- What is it about this company that's making me want to look outside?
- If I leave this organization, what are my long-term career opportunities elsewhere?
- What will I have to give up (that I love about this place) if I leave?
- What benefits and perks will I give up?
- Am I taking charge of my career, or am I just escaping?

> *I've always escaped—the minute I got bored, or had a tough boss, or wasn't getting what I wanted. This time I'm not escaping. I've done my homework and know I'm suited for and ready to own my own business. I'm leaving with information and eyes wide open.*

Before you choose this option, read the last chapter, "But If You Must Leave."

***

Expanding your career options means considering moves you may not have taken seriously before.

See what you could gain by moves other than *up.* Consider multiple goals—simultaneously.

HIRE: Are You on Board?

The hiring process does not end when you land the job. You need to get on board effectively in the first months and then stay on board. Continually marketing yourself within your own organization is vital to your success and satisfaction.

Someone wanted you here. On your first day of work they said, "Here's your badge [key, uniform, time card, ID, password, business card, cubicle]. Enjoy."

Wait. What happened to the welcoming committee and the orientation? If the team or organization you joined has provided a wonderful welcome, a comprehensive orientation, and periodically checks on your happiness level, you are fortunate. But if they haven't, don't dismay and don't wait. Pull yourself on board before you go overboard.

Build Bridges, Not Gangplanks

To get on board, you'll need to understand the job requirements, the culture, the standards, the policies and procedures, the key players, the business, the mission, the vision, and the values. That's a lot to learn.

The following checklist should start you thinking about what you need to know. (Note: Even if you've been in your organization for years, you might be able to get more on board.)

If You Can't Check It Off, Check It Out:

_ I can describe what's expected of me in this job.
_ I can describe the responsibilities of the people I work with most frequently.
_ I know what I need to do to fit in here.
_ I know the key written policies and procedures.
_ I've begun to learn some of the "unwritten rules."
_ I know what it takes to move ahead here.
_ I can name the responsibilities and functions of the major divisions and departments of my organization.
_ I can explain how my employer uses the results of my work.
_ I know whom to go to with questions.
_ I can describe the strategic direction my team or organization plans to take in the future.

If you can't check off some of these statements, start investigating. Read, question, connect, and reflect.

Read

You'll find information you need in newsletters, annual reports, policy manuals, and articles in periodicals. Read everything you can find about the history, the people, the organizing principles, and the policies. Visit your organization's Web site or intranet. Both hold a wealth of information.

Question

After you read, you'll be able to ask some great questions. You'll also have a good idea of whom to ask—sometimes your manager, sometimes a veteran colleague, sometimes people in other departments. For example:

Take a **trusted colleague** to lunch. Ask whether he or she is willing to help you learn more about the organization. If the answer is yes, then ask questions like these:

- What is one thing you know now that you wish you had known when you were new here?
- What are the important pieces of the history of this organization?
- Who are the people "in the know" here?
- What has been your biggest surprise? Disappointment?
- What advice would you give me about being successful in this organization?
- Who really does what around here?

> *I was completely at sea here until I asked a colleague about exactly who among the administrative assistants was responsible for what. That one little question opened up an hour-long conversation on the spot—and other conversations later—that ranged from specific policies to insider influence. And no wonder I wasn't clicking with*

> *the administrative assistants. For weeks and weeks, I had been asking them to help in ways that weren't even remotely in their job descriptions.*

Then do the same with your **manager.** Ask questions like these:

- What major challenges does our team, department, organization face?
- What does it take to be successful here?
- What are the "land mines" I should know about?
- Who are the people I should get to know or know about?
- What are the most likely and exciting opportunities for our organization in the future?
- How do my teammates' work responsibilities mesh with mine?

These conversations will help you understand the organization you've joined. And that understanding will help you fit.

Connect

Join people for lunch. Attend staff meetings. Volunteer for task forces. Make friends at work. You'll learn from these connections and you're more likely to feel like you fit—in the job, team, or organization.

Reflect

Think about all you've learned from colleagues, your boss, your reading. What do you want to learn about next? What will you read and with whom will you talk? The on-boarding process has no finite end.

A Never-Ending Story

Today it would clearly be a mistake to believe that once you're hired, you're safe. Downsizing and reorganization will often force you to compete for your own job. The truth is, you are, in essence, rehired by your boss, team, and organization every day. So, would you hire you? To be able to answer yes, you'll need to continually do the following:

- **Perform:** Make yourself indispensable (or close to it) by consistently doing good work, developing your skills, and dealing effectively with others. Build a reputation of someone who can be counted on—in good times and bad.

  My boss told me, before the recent downsizing, that I would not be laid off, even though my department would lose several good people. He said that everyone agreed that they needed ten more people like me. Good performance doesn't guarantee security, but it sure helps!

- **Prepare:** Develop an internal résumé and keep it updated. Where has your career taken you? What have your key accomplishments been? (Quantify them.) How up-to-date are your skills? What unique qualities and abilities do you bring to your job? How's your internal network?

  My boss showed me résumés of recent hires. I couldn't believe how résumés have changed over the years. I updated mine and included examples of successes, including money I saved the organi-

zation and new customers I won. I got a promotion, and, while the résumé wasn't the only reason, it did show that I was current and competitive.

- **Package:** Consider your self-presentation and your reputation in the organization. How do others see you? (Do they see you at all?)

  I asked a friend at work to tell me how I'm viewed by others in the organization. I asked her to give me five adjectives (and not all positives!) she's heard or thinks others would use to describe me. She did it. (What a good friend). Now I know my reputation a little better. I can decide to change it if I want.

- **Promote:** Launch a low-key internal marketing campaign. How can you promote yourself in your own organization (without bragging)? How can you interact more with others? How can you make your accomplishments more visible?

  I never bragged about my accomplishments. I figured if I did good work, everyone would know. I don't believe that anymore. I now send a note or e-mail to my boss every time I have a success. I do it in the spirit of "keeping him informed," but I know it serves me well, too. I recently won an award for outstanding customer service, and I think keeping my boss informed helped me get it!

***

Don't wait for your boss or others to orient, welcome you, or market you internally. Do it yourself. Bringing yourself onboard and truly "finding the fit" can be challenging but pays off in your success and satisfaction. Do your homework and learn as much as you can about the organization you've joined. Then perform, prepare, package, and promote yourself. Don't leave your own job fit to happenstance.

Seen in a Krispy Kreme donut shop in St. Louis, MO.

INFORMATION: Plug Yourself In

Even as kids we knew that information was power. We told secrets. I'll tell him, but not her—that makes me powerful. As effective adults, we still want and, in fact, *need* to be in the *information loop.* Why? Because accurate, timely information enables us to:

- Feel like valued members of our teams.
- Be excited about our roles and motivated to do great work.
- Make choices about our careers.
- Initiate actions that keep our own work on the cutting edge.
- Understand the culture and politics of our workplaces.

Are you *in the loop?* Do you have the real story about what's going on? In a perfect world, your manager and organization leaders would keep you in the know, especially during times of major change. But it's not a perfect world—yet. For many reasons, you may not be getting the information you need to be satisfied and successful. If that's the case, don't wait for someone else to fill you in. Take charge, *plug in,* and get more information.

In or Out of the Loop?

Have you ever felt like the last to know? That's how I felt when I picked up the Sunday paper and read that the store where I worked had been sold to a giant chain. I've never felt so out of the loop, before or since.

You May Be Out of the Loop If:

- You see substantial change (reorganization, new leadership, downsizing, position changes) but don't know why it's happening or what it means.
- You meet silence or discomfort when you ask about the future.
- Others seem to understand organization culture and politics that leave you clueless.
- Your best source of news about your workplace is the media.

If you're out of the loop, don't wait for someone else to be your informant. Do it yourself.

Build Your Network

I realized that I lived in a vacuum. I ate lunch in my office every day, never went to office parties, and seldom even strolled down the hallway or took breaks with colleagues. I'm not antisocial, just a focused, hard worker.

The problem is, I was missing out on critical information about almost everything in the organization. I was one of the last to know about a major change that impacted my team in a big way. Since then, I'm determined to get in the loop.

To Build Your Network:

- Ask people from your team and others out to lunch.
- Travel with colleagues to meetings across town or out of town.
- Attend company or unit social functions, even when you don't have to.
- Listen for clues about the culture and politics of the place.

Do Your Homework

- Read the company newsletters and annual reports.
- Scan the Internet, professional journals, business magazines, and newspapers for industry news and trends.
- Find out about the background of the new CEO or VP. If your boss or colleagues don't know, search the latest company newsletter or homepage for a bio. If your organization has neither, ask around. Someone is bound to know.

Be a Detective

List a few specific questions you have about the organization and its operations. For example, "What is the plan for staffing of this department two years from now?" or "What new products or services are being considered?"

- Ask these questions of your boss and some veteran colleagues to gain their perspectives.
- Talk to people who have left the organization; ask why they resigned.
- Use the Internet. Try sites like Vault.com that capture information from the electronic "water cooler."
- Listen to the latest rumor. There could be a grain of truth in it. Don't take it at face value but as a starting point for your detective work.

Watch the Bouncing Ball

Staying in the loop could be a full-time job in this fast-paced work world. Just when you think you have a handle on the latest scoop, top management turns over—again. Or the company gets acquired. People you trust give conflicting answers when you ask them about goals. Colleagues who are well positioned to know things admit that they only have rumors, not information, about future direction.

> *My boss is great about keeping us updated. Last week he said the latest news is that we're no longer up for sale. We breathed a sigh of re-*

> *lief. This week he said, "Never mind. It's changed. We are up for sale." He has tried to teach us that the constant changes aren't always as crazy as they seem. They're a part of doing business today.*
>
> *I am constantly asking my boss—and others—what's the latest scoop? It really is like watching a bouncing ball.*

Remember that your goal is to get information that allows you to make the most of your job. Information is a key ingredient to your success and satisfaction.

Beware the Rumor Mill

You might think you're in the loop, when actually you've plugged into the rumor mill. What we know about humans is that in the absence of information *we make it up.* Here's how it can go:

> Senior leaders think, "It's too early to tell them."
> Employees think, "The silence must mean it's pretty bad."
> Senior leaders think, "This news is too frightening—we'd better wait."
> Employees think, "They're moving the company to Panama."

Before you know it, the rumor has spread and people are busy updating their résumés or packing their bags.

The most recent rumor might, in fact, be reality. Or, it could be far from it! Take rumors to your boss or other great information sources. Check them out before you buy them or do *anything* based on them.

Close to the Vest

You know they have information they're not sharing. But why wouldn't they share? Because they might:

- Know you'll spread it—for good or bad.
- Be concerned about how you'll take the news.
- Think you're not interested or the news will distract you.
- Think it's bound to change soon anyway.
- Be under strict instructions *not to share.* Sensitive information could include things like financial data that affect the firm, salary data, legal matters, personal plans about resignation or retirement, succession ideas for who will step in next, or staffing or downsizing plans.
- Be just too busy.

When they hold it close to the vest, you might be able to get just a little more information if you explain that you and others already have some vague idea about what's going on. Or that your curiosity isn't idle—it's real concern for the organization. Or that the building rumor mill is more distracting than accurate information would be. It's worth a try. Or ask *when* the information might be available.

Afraid you'll appear pushy? That's a legitimate concern. If your boss resists your honest attempt to get information, let it go! And be patient with managers who would like to tell you all they know but aren't at liberty to do so. You may find yourself in a similar situation someday.

Give Information, Too

Think about the last time you gave information to your boss, your colleagues, or a senior leader. What did they do with it? Hopefully they listened and, at least occasionally, made some change based on it.

> *I volunteered to attend a few patient care conferences, meetings where every aspect of the patient's needs and care are discussed. Nurse aides weren't usually included because our managers thought we were too busy or not interested in attending. It was strange, though, because no one else has as much contact with the patients as the aides. We often know best what they want and need.*
>
> *In the first conference I explained why one patient should be going to the dining room instead of eating in her room. I talked about her recent physical and emotional progress, and said I thought we should try it for a week. The charge nurse heard me out and immediately changed the patient care plan. The patient is doing so well, and her family is thrilled. They thanked me for caring enough to get involved.*

Now I'm invited to every patient care conference. I can give my input and then leave, or stay for the entire meeting, whichever I prefer. We all win. The nursing staff gets critical information they need. The patients get better care. And I feel more valued because the managers listen and act on my suggestions. I've also become more aware of the organization's procedures and philosophy of care, now that I'm in the loop.

Your story may not have the happy ending this one did. But don't give up. Your good ideas deserve, and need, to be heard. Offer your suggestions, ideas, and information. In the process, you'll find others share information with you.

***

Both giving and getting information is key to getting more of what you want at work.

Seen at a dry cleaner's in Chaplin, SC.

JERK: Work with One?

The work is great, you like the organization and your teammates, and the pay is good. If it weren't for this one person, you'd be happy. But unfortunately, you work with a jerk.

Whether jerks come into your life in the form of bosses, teammates, or clients, their very existence can cause you to want to do something drastic, like jumping ship. Don't do it—at least not yet. And don't wait for someone else to fix it. There are things *you* can do to improve your situation if you work with a jerk.

Dozens of people told us that the jerks they know exhibit behaviors like these:

Intimidating

Slamming doors, yelling

Withholding praise

Belittling

Acting superior, smarter

Withholding information

Acting arrogant

Stealing credit or the spotlight

Not listening

Demanding perfection

Acting sexist/racist

Acting above the rules

Humiliating or embarrassing

Blaming

Betraying trust

Having "sloppy" moods

Motivating by fear

Setting impossible deadlines

Breaking promises

Not caring

Distrusting

Micromanaging

Research about our "emotional wiring" supports what we already know intuitively. We are affected by others' feelings and certainly by their behaviors. That's not because we're somehow weak but because we are connected to others' emotions in a profound way—whether we like it or not.

(*Note:* We use the pronouns *he, him,* and *his* throughout this chapter, just to simplify the writing, *not* because men have the corner on jerklike behaviors. You'll be pleased (or dismayed) to know that jerks are found among people of all ages, cultures, professions, and, most definitely, both genders.)

> *He had "sloppy moods." You know, he'd have a fight with his wife, or write a big check to the IRS the night before, and then come to work in a terrible mood. The problem was, he'd slop that mood all over us. I tried to not let it get me down, but it was almost impossible.*

If this were your problem, how could you deal with it—and him? You could...

Alter, Accept, or Avoid

Here's how each of those actions and activities could play out.

Alter

To *alter* means to make different, without changing into something else. So, when you alter a negative situation with someone at work, you're not trying to change the person—just the behavior.

> *I was at my wits end with "sloppy mood" guy. I decided to talk to him. I was so nervous about it that I got some advice from a couple of friends in our company. They all agreed I should talk with him, and they helped me figure out how to approach him.*
>
> *I asked to meet with him about improving my effectiveness at work and our work relationship. I took a deep breath, then said I needed his help with something. I went on to explain that when he seemed down or depressed, I allowed his behavior to affect my whole day. I actually felt down, too. I asked if we could work together to come up with some alternative ways of working together. I said that I'd be open to changes, too, if that would enhance our work relationship.*
>
> *We talked for over an hour. I know he was shocked (maybe a little hurt or angry, too). He honestly had no idea that his moods could affect anyone else so profoundly. He said they had nothing to do with me and that he valued our working relationship.*
>
> *Our solution for now is that he will try to be more aware of when he's having a bad day (or*

week). He knows he needs quiet time when he's feeling like that, so we agreed he'll give me a signal (like a closed office door), or he'll just tell me that he needs some space. If he gets that, he thinks his moods won't "slop" on me.

So I'm hopeful. We're going to give it a try and then meet again in a few weeks. We agreed we'll keep modifying this plan until it works for both of us.

To *alter,* try this:

- Get advice from savvy people who've dealt with these kinds of situations before. Practice your conversation with them.
- Speak up! Gather your courage and *talk* to the person with jerklike behaviors. Ask for some specific change and be clear about why you'd like to see the change happen (to increase your effectiveness, create a better work relationship, be more productive, reduce stress). Make sure your reasons all focus on improving work.
- Alter *your* behavior as a way of changing *his.* See what happens.
    - Ask if he needs something different from you and make agreements you can both modify later, if necessary.
    - Instead of disengaging, try putting in 25 percent more effort on the next shared project.
    - Try new approaches, give more compliments, be more supportive, and remind yourself to react differently to his actions.

Accept

To accept means to receive willingly; to give admittance or approval to; to regard as proper, normal, or inevitable.

> *I've worked with this guy for three years now. His condescending attitude used to drive me nuts. I've learned how to deal with it—and him. He's a great guy in so many ways, and the more I've learned about him—his home situation, his background—the more I've learned to accept him, warts and all. I think the good outweighs the bad.*
>
> ***I do not like this person. I must get to know him better.***
>
> —Abraham Lincoln

To *accept,* try this:

- Make a list of everything you like about him. If it's a longer list or it has more important items than the "jerklike" behavior list, you might just decide to accept him for who he is, warts and all.
- Be exceedingly curious. Go to coffee or lunch and talk about work or life or both. Try to understand where he's coming from. Try thinking, "Isn't that interesting?" when his perspective differs from yours.
- Tell him what you appreciate about him—thank him when he *does it right.* You'll reinforce the behaviors you hope he'll repeat.

Avoid

To *avoid* means to depart or withdraw from; to leave; to keep away from. So, one key in avoiding a jerk is to stay out of his way.

> *I love my job. I have autonomy and have great people working for and with me. The only problem is one of my short-tempered colleagues. We do not get along at all. I've managed to stay off the teams he's on and avoid him most of the time. It may not be an ideal situation, but for now it works fine for both of us.*

To *avoid* a jerk at work, creatively manage your schedule, your projects, or your social activities so that your paths seldom cross.

—And—

Have hope. Jerks move on. The next colleague (or client or boss) could be a favorite!

What If the Jerk Is Your Boss?

The same suggestions apply, even though the stakes may be higher and some of the strategies trickier. (It can be hard to *avoid* your boss, although we heard of a manager who mastered the technique. His boss worked in another country.)

And remember, the strategies you learn to use in trying to work with a jerklike boss will serve you well, here or in countless other work (or life) situations.

You might want to check out the Jerk Survey on our Web site, www.keepem.com, where hundreds of people have signed on to say which jerklike behaviors bother them most. The top two at the time of this printing were belittling people in front of others and telling lies.

Who, Me?

A quick look at the first-page checklist in this chapter and then in the mirror is a good idea. Do you think *you* might accidentally, occasionally exhibit any jerklike behaviors? If you're not sure, ask a friend, your kid, your partner, or your spouse. Then work to reduce those behaviors. Your colleagues, customers, boss, employees, friends, and family will notice. They might even thank you.

And, by the way, in what ways are you a jerk to yourself? Do you ever catch yourself belittling *you,* withholding praise, not caring, or self-blaming? Do you set impossible deadlines and then ridicule yourself when you fail to meet them? You get the idea. While you're working on any jerklike behaviors, be sure to put a screeching halt to those you inflict on yourself!

***

Rather than being a jerk's victim, decide what you'll do to alter, accept, or avoid him or the situation. You may not be able to rid your

workplace of jerks, but you can dramatically reduce their impact on you!

Seen in a coffee shop in Seattle, WA.

KICKS: Are We Having Fun Yet?

When was the last time you had a good laugh at work?

- Last year?
- Last month?
- Last week?
- Yesterday?

If your answer is yesterday, you're probably smiling as you read this. If you can't remember, you may work in a fun-free zone.

Caution—Fun-Free Zone

Somehow three of us stepped out of our offices at the same time, met in the hallway, and began chatting. I don't even remember what we began laughing about, but all three of us were really laughing (not very quietly). Our boss stepped out of his office furious and red-faced and said, "Is this what I'm paying you for?" Most of us left within six months. Who wants to work for a fun squelcher?

For many people, fun provides a welcome (healthy) relief from sometimes serious, stressful, time-crunched work lives. If fun at work is high on *your* priority list and you see your department, team, or organization as a "fun-free zone," you could be tempted to bolt. Don't do it. And don't wait for your boss or the VP of Fun (some companies have one!) to cheer up your workplace. Take charge, get creative, and *inject* more fun into your work.

> *One Friday, a bunch of us were working late and grumbling about everything, including the condition of the two fourth-floor restrooms. It finally dawned on us—we can change that. The next Saturday, the men took charge of the women's room and the women took charge of the men's room! Talk about creativity. We used color, murals, bizarre drapes, and countertop knick-knacks. The women's room walls now have prints of our company annual report covers framed by toilet seats. The back of the men's room door has a framed list titled "A Dozen Best Times to Take a Restroom Break." After the laughter-filled unveiling, we all went out for dinner and came up with ideas for the next fun-fest.*

OK, that might not work in your organization. Or it might not fit your definition of fun. What does?

> *I've been an administrative assistant for fifteen years. I get a kick out of doing my boss's PowerPoint presentations and surprising him with some unexpected animation or sound effects. He*

loves the result, and I get to exercise my creativity.

Or how about these forms of fun?

The day-to-day laughter my colleagues and I shared—mostly about small things.

***

We decorated my boss's office for his birthday. We used five bags of confetti from the shredding machine.

Spontaneous after-work trips to the local pizza parlor.

***

Verbal sparring with my brainy, funny colleagues.

***

We had a huge project, a tight deadline, and we had to work all night. I wouldn't want to do that often, but we had a good time, laughs in the middle of the night, and a thrill when we finished the project.

Whether you're an administrative assistant, a *barista* in a coffee shop, or a design engineer, you have opportunities for fun at work. Do you go for them?

You Go First

If you want to have fun, take charge. Be the first to hang a dartboard in the office, investigate the possibility of joining the league of office softball teams, or suggest a goldfish bowl theme for the re-decoration of the lounge.

> *We had been working long days (and a few nights) and decided we needed a break. A few of us asked the boss for a small contribution to host a picnic on Saturday at a local park. We asked people to come prepared to share their favorite hobbies—even give a few lessons if they wanted. Not only did we have a lot of fun, but we learned things about our teammates we never would have guessed. One guy played in a rock band, and another was a ham radio champion!*
>
> *Think little:* Small, no-cost activities can increase levity.
>
> *Think light:* Word games, jokes (appropriate ones) are good tension relievers.
>
> *Think creative:* Try something innovative. You do it in work all the time—try it in play.

If you want to initiate a little fun in the workplace, keep these two lists from *301 Ways to Have Fun at Work* in mind:

Top Ten Most Popular Foods

1. Cookies (the overwhelming choice)
2. Pizza

3. Doughnuts
4. Ice cream
5. Popcorn Cake
7. M&Ms
8. Pretzels (to go with the beer)
9. Candy bars
10. Beer (champagne, wine)

Top Ten Most Popular Office Toys

1. Koosh balls
2. Nerf guns
3. Nerf balls
4. Silly Putty
5. Frisbees
6. Pez dispensers
7. Slinky
8. Tinkertoys
9. Yo-yos
10. Pogo sticks or hula hoops

Now you're armed and dangerous!

***

Don't wait for someone else to be your cruise director. If having kicks at work matters to you, add "creating fun" to your unwritten job description. Think about what you really like to do. Invite others to join you. See what an injection of fun does for your feelings about your job.

Seen in a wine bar in Chicago.

LINK: Build the Connection

Most of us treasure our connections. Linking with others brings us joy and adds immensely to our capability and success—in life and at work. Our research tells us that one of the top three reasons people stay with their organizations is because of other "great people." Do the people you work with add to your satisfaction?

> *The competition was constantly coming after us—and they paid 20 percent more than my organization paid. Some people thought I was crazy to say, "No, thanks," every time the enticing offer came in. But I felt like I could never replace the camaraderie of my team. They were the smartest, nicest, most fun colleagues I'd ever had.*

When we say *link,* we mean teamwork, collaboration, interaction, sharing, information, coordination, and networking. All these activities are vital in this high-speed, high-tech, ever-changing world of work.

Missing Links

Although some workers actually can survive for years in isolated jobs, they are as rare as real hermits. Most of us need that good feeling of being connected to other colleagues, other work functions, the larger goals of the organization, or perhaps a community of people outside the organization.

Are those links missing for you? Why? You can feel disconnected in your organization if:

- you don't "click" or have much in common with others on your team;
- you are the only one who performs your function—or even really understands it;
- you work with documented information more than with people;
- you perform most of your work electronically, seldom interacting with others in person;
- the culture of your organization is competitive and noncollaborative.

If the *links* are missing, don't wait for others to build them for you. Take the initiative. Linking to others will undoubtedly help you get more of what you want at work.

I am he as you are we and we are all together.

—John Lennon and Paul McCartney

Link in Your Own Backyard

The most immediate and obvious links are built into your work in one of two ways:

- Linking to the organization
- Linking to the team or unit

To extend the link to your organization, you need to know more about its purpose and plans and understand how your own work fits the big picture. You can increase this combination of knowing and understanding in the following ways:

- Reading annual reports, newsletters, and policy manuals.
- Asking your colleagues about recent history—how things were organized, how people got where they are now.
- Learning about people in other departments and their work. Ask to attend interdepartmental meetings.
- Establishing communication links (even informal, over the water cooler) with people from inside and outside your unit.
- Finding cross-functional committees or task forces that might help your unit. Suggest to your manager that you would make the time to participate on one.
- Finding out how your company's products are viewed in the marketplace.

> *I've worked for a medical equipment manufacturing company for over a year, but I wasn't exactly sure what we made, or what difference we made to anyone. That may sound crazy, but I'm in the accounting department, and we are consumed by the day-to-day tasks. I asked my supervisor to explain more about the company's products. He did, and then he suggested I attend an*

upcoming "all-hands" meeting, where the CEO of a large local hospital would be speaking.

That CEO brought with him a patient whose life was saved by our state-of-the-art medical equipment. My work has not changed a bit, but my attitude has. I'm so proud of what this company does.

And what about linking to your team or unit? It could simply mean stepping out of your own space and getting to know others nearby.

Consider:

- Asking a colleague to partner with you on a project. (You might need to sell your manager on the idea.)
- Finding a more senior person in your department with a good track record and good visibility, who can act as your mentor. (Linking to a mentor may also create support for your career advancement.)
- Communicating with people in your unit at least some of the time by the "bump into" technique—face-to-face rather than only by e-mail.
- Participating on the office sports team.
- Helping out on the next office social function.
- Determining ways in which work could be organized more collaboratively. Get feedback on your ideas from colleagues; then take them to your manager.

The graphics division of our small textbook publishing firm was set up so that the director met with editors and then passed along their needs to one of us graphic artists. We'd each then work in isolation, sending ideas back through our director to editors. We had no idea how our graphics were received or what was coming next, and we had no idea about what our colleagues were doing.

This was not stimulating to our creativity. Finally, a newly hired graphic artist told our director that at her previous job the graphic artists worked in teams assigned to groups of editor "clients." She explained some of the resulting productivity gains. Our director liked the idea that he could do less go-between work and more balancing of our workloads. Then he convinced the editors of the productivity savings. Now I'm part of a team I really feel connected with, and we're doing some cutting-edge work.

Link to the Outside

Other good sources of links can come from outside the organization, in the form of linking to:

- your professional community and
- your local community.

To establish valuable links to other professionals in your line of work, be sure to do the following:

- Report to your manager, and others who might want to know about your findings from attending a professional conference, even if it's just a small local seminar. Offer to hold a short briefing session at your next staff meeting.
- Discover who else in your unit or organization might already belong or want to join your profes-

sional association. Plan to attend meetings together.

- Join the regional group or a special "practice area" of your professional organization. Often, more ideas and information get exchanged in small groups.
- Find out about professional groups you may be unaware of that your colleagues have joined.
- Check your company's policy on paying professional association dues and travel. If it's not a company policy, ask your manager if such membership is possible. Or join on your own. (Don't let your company's noncommitment stop you. Besides, it could be tax-deductible!)

Community service and local associations often are good ways to interact with your colleagues and make a contribution together, sometimes in the name of your company. You can try these ideas:

- Investigate the need for volunteer work—such as highway clean-up, needy families, local schools, and hospitals. Find outside opportunities to share your skills with others.
- Talk to your manager about a department-wide effort, and learn how the company will get credit for the work.
- Involve your colleagues in community projects. "Who wants to help build a house this Saturday, followed by pizza?"
- Consider inviting people from another department to join you in an outside service project.

- Join a local Toastmasters' club, a great place for skill building and networking—combined.

To Get a Link, Be a Link

The Latin expression *quid pro quo* means "something for something" or, in a more contemporary translation, "If you do something for me, I'll do something for you." If linking is only used to network on your own behalf, it will become one-sided and self-serving.

> *I found the perfect team and a few really good work partners when I moved from development to sales. I so badly needed information and encouragement in this new line of work that I absorbed everything they said to me and did for me like a sponge. Then, after a few months, these same colleagues started being more distant, and I slowly started feeling disconnected. Luckily, one caring colleague told me, "You've been observing and taking things in, without giving much back." What a wake-up call! Since then I've started contributing what I know, and I can see the connections beginning to build again.*

Direct reciprocity doesn't have to be the only way this works. A movie based on the book *Pay It Forward* suggested that individuals offer to "give back" by giving to three other people who need help.

- Offer an immediate thank-you when you feel you've been given a good connection. Then go beyond the thanks by spending time networking with others who can benefit from your experience or expertise.

- Listen to what topics your colleagues are interested in, and when you come across pertinent information, share it with them.

Eventually, everybody wins. Imagine working with people who hold this kind of philosophy. Perhaps you could begin this in your own department.

***

Don't wait for your boss or others to include you or build the connections for you. Step forward and strengthen the bonds between you and others *inside* and *outside* your organization.

Seen in a restaurant in Maui.

MENTOR: Make Your Own Match

What is a mentor? And who needs one? According to *Webster's,* a *mentor* is a trusted counselor or guide, a tutor or coach. Given that definition, we *all* need one. Actually, we need many, throughout our work lives.

Does your organization *provide* mentors for new hires, high potentials, or special leadership programs? If they do, and they *offer* you one, say yes. But if they don't have formal mentoring programs or you're not included, don't wait for someone to offer to mentor you. Identify what you want, and then seek those with the wisdom you need. You *will* find them, right where you work.

> *I searched for a mentor. I wanted someone who had "been there, done that" and who could advise me as I grew in my career. When I asked a highly respected woman to be my mentor, she gave me some great advice. She suggested that I find several people to serve in the role. She agreed to guide me but felt others could provide some critical skills training and insights that she*

couldn't offer. So, I created a type of "brain trust," made up of smart, talented people who can teach and counsel me, using their skills and experience, as I grow. They've been my mentors for the past three years and are making a phenomenal difference in my confidence and competence.

How can you begin your search for mentors?

Search for a Sage

A great mentor for someone else might not be the match for you (and vice versa). The first step is to determine what you want or need. **Interview yourself:**

- What skills or traits do I want to develop? Who could best teach me that?
- Do I want to learn from someone similar to or different from me?
- Do I want someone I already know to be my mentor? Or do I want to expand my network by having a mentor I don't know?
- How much time do I want to spend?

Once you know what you want in a mentor, start *looking.*

Look for mentors in your own department and beyond. Candidates for the job will surface. *And your mentors may not be senior to you.* They could be older *or* younger, higher *or* lower in rank, doing work similar to yours *or* very different.

Start your search by:

- Listening for **stories.** Who tells meaningful (and honest) stories about their own successes and failures?
- Asking for **advice.** Actively listen and decide whose advice makes the most sense to you.
- Looking for the **"real scoop."** Who knows how things *really* work in your organization?
- Observing as others **relate** and interact. Who is respected and admired?
- Sharing your ideas and requesting feedback. Notice the quality of the feedback and the style of the **feedback** provider.

Multiple Mentor Moments

Some people think of mentoring as one-on-one relationships, stretched over long periods (sometimes years). In today's world, that form of mentoring is rare. Things change too fast, people move too often, and mentors are busy people.

The new form of mentoring looks different but is just as effective, if not more. It involves having *multiple mentors,* each of whom teaches, coaches, or guides you in different ways and at different times. Your goal is to create a wide web of these relationships and contacts that you can use throughout your career.

Another variation to consider is the idea of *mentoring moments.* Instead of being mentored over a long period of time, you are provided just what you need in that moment, that week, or that month. Once you learn what you need from that mentor, you move on.

You can open yourself to *multiple mentor moments* (try saying that fast three times) if you look for people who are willing to:

- **Sponsor:** Someone in a position of power or authority who can help increase your visibility and your ability to reach your goals.
- **Teach:** Someone who can help you learn a new skill by instructing, demonstrating, and/or giving feedback as you try new things.
- **Nurture:** Someone who can listen and constructively challenge your ideas, frustrations, and doubts and encourage and support your decisions by being a good sounding board.
- **Connect:** Someone who can help you build relationships by introducing you to others; someone who can include you in activities that give you access to others.
- **Advise:** Someone who can help you understand the organization, its changes, and the implications.
- **Inform:** Someone who is in the information loop and is willing to share the scoop with you; someone who has the history and savvy to understand the politics and power in your organization.

How would someone in one or more of these roles impact your workplace satisfaction?

> *By the time I'd been there a year, I could see that veterans had much to share and could be instrumental in my success every day and in the*

long run. I knew they were busy, but I also knew that if I didn't approach them, they wouldn't approach me. So I bit the bullet and asked for a specific amount of time from several different people. I learned so much because each one had such a different view.

Focus Your Mentor by Focusing Yourself

Before you meet with prospective mentors, focus on what you want from them. The more specific you can be, the easier it is for them to help you. (No busy person wants a giant, open-ended, vague request from you.) To start getting focused, fill in these blanks:

I want to learn _____.
My long-term career goals are _____.
My role models in the company include _____ because _____.
I'd like my organization to take better advantage of this strength: _____
A difficult lesson I still struggle with is _____.
My current network includes _____.
It needs to be extended in this way _____,
Because _____.

How did you do? If you had difficulty filling in the blanks, you're not alone. Most people need to ask and answer questions like these before they can make the most of a mentoring relationship. The payoff is worth the effort.

Do Your Part

Will you be a good mentee (receiver of mentoring)? To find out, take this quiz.

Mentee Qualities Quiz	Yes	Some what	No
I'm open to and accept responsibility for learning.			
I like to ask (and answer) tough questions.			
I enjoy getting advice and feedback (even negative feedback) from others I respect.			
I'm good at separating advice that fits from advice that doesn't fit.			
I act on ideas that will stretch and develop me.			
I'm responsible and have great follow-through.			
I believe I can learn something from almost everyone.			
I have the time, energy, and commitment to work with mentors.			

If you answered no to several statements, you may not be *quite* ready for mentors. Think about it, talk about it with others who've had mentors, and see what you can do to shift the no's to yes's.

If you answered yes, you're ready to conduct your own sage search. As you do, here are a few words of wisdom from those who've done it successfully:

- Be proactive in your search for mentors. Don't wait for them to come to you.
- Seek out daily doses of mentoring. Look for those moments every day when you have the opportunity to learn a lesson, receive feedback, or just listen.
- Create a plan of action for your mentors that includes a definition of what you need from them, how often you'll get together, what types of activities you'll do together, and the roles you hope they will play.
- Cast a wide net. Regard every person with whom you come into contact as a potential mentor.
- Remember to give back! Everyone who mentors you deserves to be asked, "What can I do for you in return?"

***

Mentors can accelerate your learning, build your confidence, and broaden your network. Don't wait for your organization to assign you a mentor, and don't fret if no one seeks

you out. Mentors are everywhere. You just may need to seek them yourself.

Seen on a jogger in Laguna Beach, CA.

NUMBERS: Assess Your Worth

I need a raise. No, I deserve a raise. I'm working harder than ever before, and I'd like to be compensated for it.

—Almost everyone we know

Show Me the Money

In the film *Jerry Maguire,* one of Jerry's clients, like millions of workers around the world, continues to ask for his fair share (or more). Our paychecks, in addition to buying food and shelter, become a critical yardstick for how much our employers value us. It makes sense we'd want more.

I want *more.* Does that mean

- I'm not paid enough for the work I do? My pay is non-competitive or inadequate to live on? I need/want more money to buy things, pay my rent, take a trip, or surprise my kids?

—or does it mean

- I don't feel rewarded, valued, or appreciated enough?

Often what we think is all about money has very little to do with money.

Is It about the Money?

Do you need to be

- thanked,
- included,
- or recognized

more than you need more money?

If the answer is yes, go immediately to the "Rewards" chapter or back to the one on "Dignity," and then read "Ask" (again). If the answer is no, read on.

> ***Every morning I get up and look through the Forbes list of the richest people in America. If I'm not there, I go to work.***
>
> —Robert Orben

Are you paid enough for what you do? How do you know? **Quiz yourself:**

- Others with similar jobs, abilities, and experience in my industry and geography are compensated more. (Yes/No/Not sure)
- Benefits, bonuses, and other monetary rewards are lower here than in comparable jobs. (Yes/No/Not sure)

- Recent raises have not kept up with cost of living increases or what the competitors are doing. (Yes/No/Not sure)
- Also, _____

How many times did you answer "not sure"? What additional beliefs or assumptions did you add to the list?

Investigate and Calculate

Depending on your quiz results, you may need to explore the numbers before you decide to ask for more. Look at salary comparisons on Web sites (such as www.salary.com). Also, contact professional organizations in your field that track salaries. Or, the next time a recruiter calls, ask about competitive salaries.

And most importantly: What you are paid is not simply about your salary. Be sure to calculate the value of your benefits:

- Health insurance
- Life and disability insurance
- Paid leave
- Professional development reimbursement
- Compensatory time
- Employer contributions to retirement plans
- Cars, phones, and computers your organization provides
- Bonuses
- Uniforms
- Lunch programs

Also remember to include the harder-to-calculate (but important) benefits of your current job, such as these:

- Learning opportunities your organization offers
- Conferences you are able to attend
- Books, periodicals, and subscriptions that you receive
- Flexibility in work schedule and the ability to telecommute

And don't forget to consider how you and your family feel about your circumstances:

- Family loves the area; good schools
- Love your job, team, freedom, flexibility
- Feel rewarded in many other ways, beyond the pay

Some Bosses Don't Have All the Information

Your boss may have no idea how your compensation compares to others, what you are worth, what you need to continue contributing to the organization—or what it would cost to replace you.

> *It sounds incredible, but when I presented my case for more pay and a more flexible schedule, I realized almost immediately that my department head had only a vague idea what I was paid or what I should be paid, given competitive salaries elsewhere!*

Fortunately, I was able to hand her a list that showed her the salary and benefits comparisons. I'd even made a chart showing our unit's salary trends over five years, compared to cost-of-living increases in our region. And, I gave her an article that detailed some flextime opportunities she had never thought about. A week later, she put wheels in motion to get me a fairly immediate bonus and a future raise. She asked me to chair an employee task force to examine work scheduling and flextime options.

Put Your Numbers to Work

People lose sleep over asking for more of almost anything—more autonomy, more vacation, more help with the work, and especially more money. In fact, some would rather leave a good job than ask for a raise! Others have no idea how to prepare.

Employee: I want a raise.
Boss: Really, why should I give you one?
Employee: I need the money.

Or

I'm worth it.

Or

I'll leave if I don't get it.

Gee, that worked out great ... *not.*

You need to plan for and then have *the big talk* with your manager. Here is some homework you could do in preparation for this meeting. Any (or all) of these numbers and information can be persuasive. Gather what you think you'll need to make your case:

- **Summarize** the comparative compensation information you collected, on a neatly typed page.
- **Review** your annual earnings (including benefits) for the past three to five years. Add detail about increasing cost of living or inflation.
- **List** your changing work tasks and responsibilities over the same time frame.
- **Consider** contributions you have made to your team, your boss, and your organization. Quantify the results whenever possible.

  I installed a new contact management system in our office. As a result, our customer contacts have increased by 40 percent over the past year, and corresponding sales have amounted to $300,000. That should impress my boss, huh?
- **Collect** past performance evaluations (skip the ho-hum ones) and all congratulatory letters you've stashed in your files.
- **Decide** what you really *want* (monetary and non-monetary).
- **Negotiate** what you'll accept, for now. Consider alternative currencies such as relief from a boring project, an opportunity to attend professional

meetings and conferences, technology upgrades, or flexibility to work from home.

My boss was clearly nervous when I came in asking for a raise. He had just been told that all raises and bonuses were put on hold while the company tried to improve its performance and profits. He said that I deserve every bit of what I was requesting and wished that he could say yes. He was thrilled when I said I understood the spot he was in and that I was definitely willing to wait a few months to revisit this discussion. Meanwhile, we agreed to some of the other things on my "want" list.

***

Assume that your organization and your manager want to keep you; it will put you in the right mind-set. If your work is good, and your skills are up-to-date, then it is most likely that they do. Managers know that talent keeps them competitive. For the most part, they want to meet your needs. You might help them do that by knowing and showing them some numbers (they might pass them along to their bosses) and by offering currencies *other* than money. As you ask, be patient with their predicament. Be collaborative. Be nondefensive. Be creative. Your professionalism will pay off in the long run.

Seen at a mall in Simi Valley, CA.

OPPORTUNITIES: They're Still Knocking

I left for a better opportunity.

—Said in thousands of exit interviews

Sometimes people say it on their way out the door just because they don't want to burn bridges. In other cases it's the truth—they leave in search of opportunities. They want to learn new skills, take on more responsibility, use cutting-edge technologies, or have other (or more) career options.

Many of their managers say, "We could have offered that. Why didn't he/she tell me?" Yes, most managers could have asked their talented people what opportunities they wanted, but most employees who left also *could have spoken up and asked for what they wanted.* If they had, they might have found just what they were looking for, right where they were.

To uncover opportunities in your organization, *tell* someone you are looking for them!

Opportunity Alert? Or Opportunity Inert?

Try this quick quiz to see how opportunity minded you are. How descriptive is each statement of you? Answer yes, somewhat, or no to each.

1. I actively "lobby" to take on challenges that are new for my position.
2. I attend more seminars, conferences, and workshops than most people in my area.
3. I read and research to keep on top of trends both in this industry and in my profession.
4. I have a lot of curiosity about others' views, opinions, and issues.
5. I not only continually increase my technical skills but also make sure my communications and presentations are always top-notch.
6. I am actively involved in professional groups relevant to my area.
7. I develop and maintain relationships at many levels throughout the organization.
8. I turn to other people as resources for my career growth.

If you answered yes to most of these questions, you are already opportunity minded and should find it easy to keep aware of favorable opportunities within the organization. If you answered somewhat or no to more than half of the questions, you may be "inert" or blind to available or potential opportunities right where you are.

If you are not as opportunity alert as you could be, it may be time to increase your ability to:

- Seek opportunities that are not readily apparent.
- See opportunities that pertain to you.
- Seize opportunities by taking action.

Seek: You Might Find

If you are good at seeking opportunities, you are constantly on the lookout. Your antennae are raised, and you are optimistic about your search. You believe opportunities do exist. Seekers will step outside their comfort zone to explore new territory. They are energetic and persistent.

> *It was well known in our organization that the task force on reviewing our health insurance benefits was not just a thankless and boring assignment. It also placed task force members in the uncomfortable position of having their carrier and benefit selections questioned by the employees.*
>
> *I realized that here was an opportunity to sharpen my ability in efficiently taking the pulse of our employee "clients" and in building consensus. And it gave me the opportunity to have influential people in other parts of the organization not only to know me but also to see how I used my skills and experience. Deciding to seek out a seat on the task force was one of my better career decisions in this organization.*

Which of these ways might help you find opportunities in your organization? Do you:

- Ask your colleagues or boss what upcoming projects are going to be difficult to staff?
- Read your organization's newsletter to see what management is contemplating or planning for the future?
- Have an "open line" with the appropriate human resources people concerning position openings or changes that have just occurred or are just over the horizon?
- Listen carefully to and "read between the lines" of all verbal and written updates and plans presented by executive and department management?

See: What's in Front of You and More

Vision. Perspective. Outlook. You need all of these to meet the challenge of seeing opportunities that present themselves nearly every day.

> *There's an old story about a psychologist who invites a group of four-year-olds into her office. In the middle of the floor is a large pile of manure. Each child is handed a shovel, while the psychologist watches through a one-way mirror. Four of the five children run out of the room holding their noses. One begins to dig with his shovel. When the psychologist asks*

> *why, the young boy replies, "If there's this much manure, there must be a pony in here somewhere!"*

If you are good at *seeing,* you perceive possibilities and potential in the most unlikely places and in the most unlikely people. You have the ability to look far and wide, as well as to narrow your focus sharply. You see the forest *and* the trees. And you see not just black and white but many shades of gray. You can easily create a mental picture and a clear vision of what you want. You remain open to seeing something differently than others do.

> ***Opportunities are usually disguised as hard work, so most people don't recognize them.***
>
> —Anonymous

You can increase your ability to see new opportunities by:

- Thinking creatively ("We could do this better if we got training in...").
- Seeing the other side of the question or problem ("It's not the boss; it's the rules...").
- Looking for better ("This could be a lot more interesting, if I also handled...").
- Perceiving in wide angle ("That department could use my skill in...").
- Thinking big ("This little nuisance project could be the start of...").

- Thinking beyond ("I'll check to see if other departments might...").

Seize: This Day and Beyond

Looking for and finding opportunities are relatively easy for some people. Actually seizing the opportunity can be a very different story.

Do you have a list of property or stocks you *almost* bought that have since doubled or tripled in value? Is there a degree you intended to earn or a gym you almost joined? If you are opportunity alert, you know how to seize. You grab the opportunity before it gets away. You recognize the barriers as well as your own fears. You create plans for overcoming them. Then you take action!

> *I started here as one of several computer experts in our technology support area. We answered phone calls, did network troubleshooting, and gave new program advice. I got friendly with many of my customers on the phone, and, when possible, tried to drop by their offices for face-to-face help. Soon it dawned on me: The people I visited seemed to call in less frequently; they were solving their own problems. I saw my most effective work as technology "guidance" rather than technology problem solving. That led me to an idea for a technology guidance team that does everything face-to-face. I seized the opportunity to show how a technology team, with my leadership, could be a real added value for our clients.*

My boss agreed, and I now lead a team of great people who are solving technical problems, not just troubleshooting. My work is more fun now than ever before.

You are more likely to be able to *seize* opportunities if you:

- Write out your goals, draft an action plan with potential obstacles, and draw a time line related to the new opportunity.
- Get lots of information about the opportunity. Talk to others in your organization who may have a breadth of knowledge wider than yours.
- Establish a network of colleagues and friends who can serve as your advisers. They might brainstorm solutions to the barriers or provide support.
- Make two lists: "What if" you do nothing? "What if" you take the plunge? Follow the "what ifs" to their respective conclusions and then decide: Which conclusion do you prefer?
- Watch out for naysayers and risk-averse friends. They may be *opportunity inert.*
- Avoid paralysis by analysis. Sometimes overanalyzing the opportunity is just a delay tactic in disguise.
- Face your fear and do it anyway. Push yourself to act once you've determined it's what you really want to do.

***

Everything changes, including your potential opportunities. What you seek and see today may change (even disappear) with the next reorganization or downsizing. Or another opportunity may be created in the process. Although you don't control the environment in which opportunities occur, you can control your own response. Don't wait for your boss or anyone else to hand you the next opportunity. Be flexible, keep your eyes (and ears) open, and be willing to act. Oh—and make sure that when opportunity knocks, you not only hear it but also are prepared to open the door.

Ideas are a dime a dozen. People who put them into action are priceless.

—Unknown

Seen at a personal growth seminar in the 1970s.

PASSION: It's Not Just a Fruit

I Love My Work!

Know anyone who's said that lately? Have *you* said it lately? Here are the telltale signs of having *passion-filled* work:

- The hours fly by. It's quitting time (or later) before you know it.
- You're *in the zone:* You're creative, energized, and have a sense of well-being.
- Others have trouble getting your attention; you cannot be distracted.
- You forget to eat (or sleep or shower).
- You produce phenomenal results.
- It feels more like play than work.

That could be you.

On the other hand, if the *thrill is gone,* hours seem like days, the creativity well is dry, everything distracts you, you eat constantly, you're always tired, and it definitely feels like work.

Loathing Monday is a lame way to spend one-seventh of your life.

—Unknown

Too many people expect their managers to *provide* exciting work. Yet many have never even told the boss which parts of the job they love most and what they'd like to change. How about you? Get clear about your passion, and then go after it!

Spice It

> *I love graphic arts and volunteered to start up the company newsletter. It was so well received that my boss asked if I'd continue working on future editions. I told him I'd love to do that but* **would need to hand off about 10 percent of my current workload to someone else.** *We created a solution together and now I'm turning out a first-class newsletter. I love my job!*

When we asked dozens of people about their work passions, here is some of what we heard:

- I love creating something new.
- I get a kick out of working on a great team.
- I love numbers. I'd rather work with them than with people.
- I love drawing, welding, or building something.
- My passion is for fixing anything that is broken—work processes, TVs, teams.
- I love to help someone get better at something.

What are you passionate about? As you move through a workday, notice which tasks and interactions are exciting and fun for you. Once you know what gives you a thrill, you can try to add more of it to your work routine.

> *I was so bored with my work that I was thinking about quitting. I was talking to an airplane seatmate about the job when it dawned on me: The two things I love most about work (mentoring others and solving very tricky problems) are missing in this current job.*
>
> ***I called my boss the following Monday and asked about getting more of either one of those activities.*** *He gladly handed me a huge technical problem that no else wanted to touch. Within days I had gathered a small team of people to work on it. Guess who their mentor is? I'm thrilled about work again.*

What a simple solution. Notice what's missing and then ask for it. What do you have to lose?

> ***Passions are wired into the real world more directly than our workday routines are. If you love something, you'll bring so much of yourself to it that it will create your future.***

—Francis Ford Coppola

Search for It

Sometimes the work just isn't thrilling—at least not at the moment. But there are many other reasons to stay where you are. It may take some effort and a little patience, but work you love could be around the next bend. You just need to look for it.

> *We had just completed a huge project, and I was in limbo at work. I decided to spend some time networking, talking with others about what might be happening soon. After just a few months, I learned about an exciting new project.* ***I asked my boss about it in the nick of time. Once he realized I was interested, he put me on it.*** *The thrill was back—and lasted for five years. By then, I knew the doldrums were a normal part of the ebb and flow of work. I also knew that if I was proactive and patient I'd find another exciting project in my organization.*

Don't settle for work that leaves you cold, at least not for long. Find work you're passionate about by:

- Charging up your network. Talk to anyone who'll listen. Ask what's happening—when and where. Think about how you could fit in.
- Telling people what you love to do. Remind your boss (she might have many people's passions to keep track of) and others, which work you really like and which doesn't thrill you.
- Reading the company newsletters, annual reports, and press releases. You might learn about a start-up opportunity or task force that's right up your alley.

Choose a job you love and you'll never have to work a day in your life.

—Confucius

Blend It

What if you really *love* art and you make a living as an accountant? Or football is your passion and you're a teacher? Or you love acting and you're a waitress?

> *Our waitress was vivacious and entertaining. Her enthusiasm was infectious. She stood out in contrast to some of her coworkers, for whom, clearly, the "thrill was gone."*
>
> *We told her that she seemed to love her work and asked how long she'd been doing it. She said, "For 12 years." She went on to explain that her education is in the performing arts and that she participates in local theater.* ***She said she decided to blend her acting passion with her job.*** *Every day and every table is another debut. She loves her work, and her customers love her.*

Think about it. Is there a way to blend your outside-of-work passion *with work?*

Are you passionate about:

- Cooking? Cook for your teammates.
- Decorating? Help the interior decorator for the next office "face lift."
- Music? Start up an office band.
- Sports? Coach the football (baseball, volleyball, dance) team.

- Writing? Start a company newsletter.
- Cars? Teach a car care class for coworkers.
- The stage? Offer to be master of ceremonies for the holiday party.

Get creative. Unless your passion is really "out there" (sky diving, mud wrestling), you can probably bring interest and fun to the workplace while you indulge in your favorite pastime.

There are many things in life that will catch your eye, but only a few will catch your heart. Pursue them.

—Anonymous

Request It

Look back at each of the stories in this chapter and find the **purple** text. What did you notice? These people, in search of work they loved,

- Called the boss.
- Offered options.
- Made recommendations.
- Made requests.

The boss was not left guessing. And these employees didn't sit and hope someone would hand them work they could be passionate about.

***

Sometimes it takes courage to make a change in pursuit of your passion. You might need to *ask* someone for a chance to try something new or even fail a few times in a new, *beginner* role.

Not only is having passion for your work possible; it's crucial. It enriches your life and your soul. Launch a passionate search for ways to bring together your passion and your work.

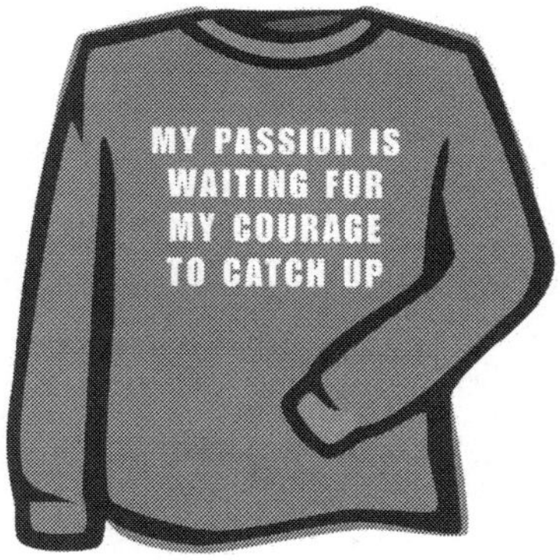

Seen at Harboryard Stadium, Bridgeport, CT.

QUESTION: Go Outside the Box

Traditions, policies, standards, rules. We count on them to provide safety and stability in our communities and workplaces. But sometimes those guidelines take on a life of their own. They multiply, they live in huge manuals, and they begin to stifle productivity and creativity.

They might also stifle your enjoyment. If you're feeling blocked—by the rules, the culture, or the boss—don't despair. There are things you can do to get out of the box you're in and get more of what you want at work.

> *My team called the organization a "ship of rules." It took dozens of signatures and often months to get the simplest request approved. We knew there had to be a better way. We got approval to try a new, more streamlined approach that we thought would save the company time and money and produce a better product, too. How could they say no to that? Our jobs are a lot more fun now, and the company*

president publicly thanked us for questioning a few of the outdated rules and procedures.

What Is This Box Made Of?

If you're feeling boxed in and want to move outside your box, you need to understand it more clearly. What are the walls composed of? What's the best escape route?

Your box may feel fairly rigid, as if the rules were made up of concrete walls. But in reality, your box could be made of one of four different materials, each with unique properties. Here is an example:

- **Concrete.** These walls represent rules that are truly rigid: *"You must have a medical degree to practice medicine in this hospital."* They cannot be broken, pushed, bent, or shattered, without risking your permanent departure. Don't hit your head against one of these walls. It will hurt. The only time it feels good is when you stop!
- **Glass.** These walls are strong, but if you hit them just the right way with just the right instrument at just the right time, they will break: *"Women will never be Supreme Court Justices."*
- **Rubber.** These walls are thick and strong but have some give. They represent rules that might be flexible, if you are willing to push hard against them: *"We must have a forty-hour week, from eight to five, five days a week."*

- **Vapor.** These walls are made up of our beliefs, assumptions, and perceptions about the rules: *"I could never learn a foreign language."* You can put your hand right through them. It doesn't take strength, just guts to take the first step through these walls.

If you examine the rules by which you operate, you will find that *few* of them are truly concrete. They just feel that way. The most overwhelming aspect of your box could be the vapor walls. Your beliefs and assumptions (about yourself, other people, the organization, the world) often prevent you from questioning the rules. In short, you may box *yourself* in.

> *I've heard of several people asking for something special, and the answer is always no—the policy manual forbids it. I thought it might be easier to quit than to ask for flextime so I could finish my college degree. I finally decided I had nothing to lose. I planned my discussion carefully, chose a good time to talk to my boss, and just went for it. I waited for the no and was shocked. The answer was yes. That was twenty-five years ago. I'm glad, and so are they, that I asked.*

What if he hadn't asked? He would have continued to assume the answer was no, continued to feel trapped, and probably would not have earned his college degree. When do you assume the answer will be no? Analyze the box you're in. Are the walls made of concrete, glass, rubber, or vapor?

Try this:

- Respect the concrete walls, or at least tread carefully. If you decide to try to break one down, have a "plan B."
- Plan your strategy for attacking the glass wall. The first female Supreme Court justice prepared thoroughly and gathered phenomenal support before she attempted to break that wall.
- Get some advice from trusted others (respected people who are question-friendly) as you push on rubber walls. If you plan to ask your boss for something radically different from the norm, chat first with people who know him and the organization's culture well.
- Eliminate the vapor walls. Sometimes you only have to shift your beliefs and challenge your assumptions to do it.

  A colleague and I worked in a rule-respecting, traditional organization. We were both starting our families and thought we'd probably have to quit our great jobs and find part-time work somewhere else. We decided to "push the envelope" and ask about job sharing. There was no precedent in the company, but we didn't let that stop us. We figured the worst was that we'd lose the jobs we were ready to quit anyway! Our manager went to bat for us, and we've been job sharing for fifteen years now. It worked for us and for them.

Be clear about expectations others have of you, and honestly evaluate your performance. Make sure you meet deadlines and deliver great results. If people trust you to perform, they'll usually tolerate (even support) your questioning of the rules.

> ***Sometimes it's better to know some of the questions than all of the answers.***
>
> —Unknown

Some Rule Breakers We've Grown to Love (Just So You Know You're Not Alone)

Think about the people who questioned the status quo or the prevailing beliefs of their time. They asked things like these:

- Why *can't* people fly?
- Why *can't* we prevent polio?
- Why *can't* we use lasers to perform surgery?
- Why *can't* we build a computer after it's ordered?
- Why *can't* we reclaim Lake Erie to its former glory?
- Why *can't* we build airplanes invisible to radar?
- Why *can't* we bring eagles back from the brink of extinction?

 and

- Why *cant* we have flextime, casual dress on Fridays, self-managed teams, child care centers, telecommuting, maternity leave, or employee ownership plans?

 Aren't you glad they asked?

***

When the rules, traditions, or policies have you boxed in, question them. See which are rigid and which might be bent or even broken.

Seen at a hotdog stand, Passaic, NJ.

REWARD: Reap Your Own

I spent hours helping him work through workplace dilemmas. Eventually, he changed careers and landed his first job as a high school teacher. Six months later he approached me at a meeting and said, "Because of you, I'm losing sleep at night." I said, "Oh, no, why is that?" He said, "I love my work so much that I wake up thinking about what I plan to do in the classroom the next day. Thank you again for all of your help."

I wasn't paid for the work I did with him. Yet I feel a tremendous sense of reward. That feeling is renewed every time he receives acclaim from his school or forwards a student's thank-you email.

Sure, money matters. Our paychecks not only help us sustain life, but they also are a measure of how much our employers (or our clients) value our work. Nonetheless, all reward experts (after thousands of studies stretched over six decades) agree that *most of us want more than money from our work.*

The best work never was and never will be done for money.

—Unknown

If you're not feeling rewarded enough, think about why. Then take heart. You can get more of the specific kinds of rewards you want, right where you are.

The Ins and Outs of Reward

You've heard about *intrinsic* rewards. They are the rewards we give ourselves. The reward could be the feeling you get when you do work that makes a difference in the world, or when you help others and watch them shine, or when, as in the Olympics, you score a perfect 10. For most people, no amount of money can match those rewards.

To see whether you're doing a good job with *intrinsic* rewards, **interview yourself:**

- How can I find more meaning in my work? Look closely. Your work matters to someone.

  I've been the janitor here for almost thirty years. We take care of elderly people who need nursing care. They deserve the best, after all they've done and given in their lives. I love my work. I help make this building beautiful and safe for the people who work here and the people who live here.

- How can I give it my best shot? If you're bringing half your heart or brain or energy to work, you're probably missing out on intrinsic rewards. Try giving your all to the next project or in the next meeting, just to see how it feels.

- How could I help someone else? Perhaps you can teach someone something you know. Help a colleague on a deadline, or serve on a committee doing charitable work. Or just make the coffee!

Good work is its own reward.

OK, so you'd also like some *extrinsic* rewards. These are the external gifts, usually from someone else to you. They can be tangible (you can touch it, feel it, bank it) or intangible (you can't touch it, feel it, bank it).

Here's something we know for sure. The leaders of your organization, right this minute (well, sometime during this year), are guessing which rewards will mean the most to you. Are they guessing right?

They may be thinking about items like these:

- More money
- A promotion
- A plaque to hang on the wall
- A reserved parking space

You might say, "Sure, thanks, I'll take more money and the plaque." Some of you would take the promotion, too, but others of you would say, under your breath, "No, thanks, that's not what rings my chimes." But, there may be other things on your want list. What are they?

What *extrinsic* rewards would you choose? Check your top five:

- An award, preferably presented in front of my peers
- A thank-you, in writing, from my boss
- A note from my boss to his boss about my excellent performance
- Frequent pats on the back
- Seeing my boss actually implement one of my ideas
- A chance to work on a really exciting, cutting-edge project
- A bonus
- A day off
- Words of praise in front of my family
- A raise
- A chance to go to lunch with senior management
- An opportunity to work with people from other parts of the company
- A chance to serve on one of the important steering committees
- A promotion
- An unscheduled upgrade in my computer or cell phone
- A change in my title
- A small memento or gift
- Trusting me enough to let me do something big—without supervision
- Some flexibility in my schedule
- A bigger cubicle or office (or one with a great view)
- More freedom or autonomy
- A seminar or training class

- A chance to represent the organization (or department) at a regional or national conference
- Gift certificates (for dinner, theater, a sporting event)
- _____ (what else?)

It isn't what you did for me; it's that you believe in me.

What did you notice about your top five choices? How many were tangible? Intangible? Which seem to matter most to you right now?

To get more of the extrinsic rewards you want from others, **try this:**

- Meet (or surpass) your objectives.
- Have a chat with your boss (see the "Ask" chapter) about the rewards you'd like. Spell it out.

  We wowed the client and won the new business. My boss was thrilled. He said, "Let's celebrate." I told him I'd love to celebrate and that I'd also like to include my family, since they had supported me during the past few weeks of hard work. He agreed. He wrote a note to my family, praising my work and thanking them for their part in our success. In the note he told them I could have the Friday I'd asked for off so I could take them on a three-day camping trip. The reward for me was huge.

- Thank them for the thanks. People will do more of what they're rewarded for. If you want more praise, recognition, or thank-you's, catch your boss (or coworker, employee, client) doing it right. Tell them how much it means to you to be noticed or thanked the way they did it.

If you like the music, thank the band.

—Unknown

- Pay it forward. Reward people in meaningful ways and ask them to do the same for others in the organization. Before you know it, it's coming back your way, and you've helped create a culture that notices and rewards people in countless valuable ways.

My father always said, "Give them flowers while they're living. Don't wait for the funeral." I don't wait. I thank people for a job well done or for giving it their best shot. I tell them what I appreciate them for. It's no surprise that I find people thanking me, too.

- Drop a few hints, just as you might before your birthday: "My favorite restaurant is the Sleeping Frog" or "I love hockey games."

Do It Yourself

Give *yourself* a reward. *Let the stroke soak.* Think about the last round of applause you received (even silent applause) for a job well done. Did you take time to soak it in, to truly enjoy it? Or did you quickly move on to the next project or task, without a pause to reflect or bask in your success? Too often we rob ourselves of the rewards that come in the form of compliments, recognition, or satisfaction of having done good work.

When you've worked hard, done a good job, or reached a goal, don't wait for someone to notice. Treat yourself. Choose from your list of favorite rewards. Go to a movie, take a friend to dinner, take a nap, ride your bike, or eat some chocolate.

***

If you're not feeling rewarded enough at work, why is that? Get clear about what's missing. Think about who could provide what you *really* want (it could even be you). Then go after it!

U.S. representative's favorite T-shirt.

SPACE: Want Some?

If you've raised a teenager (or remember being one), you know the phrase "Give me some space!" Whether you call it elbow room or freedom, think of work-related space as more control, more flexibility, more independence, more power, or more influence.

If you're feeling fenced in, overcontrolled, or frustrated by your lack of freedom, don't wait for the rules to change or for your boss to fix it. Take charge and do something to get more *space,* right where you are.

Want Outer or Inner Space?

Outer space refers to the physical world, especially your work environment. It includes the freedom or power to do things such as these:

- Design or decorate your own work area, just the way you like it.
- Work from different places, such as your home, your car, the beach.
- Take a time-out, a break, or sabbatical from work.
- Wear what you want to wear.

By *inner space,* we mean the mental and emotional space you need to feel creative and productive. It includes space to do the following:

- Be self-directed (as opposed to micromanaged).
- Manage your own time.
- Work, think, create, and produce in your own unique ways.

Which kind of space does this story illustrate?

Much of my work can be accomplished from anywhere. I'm on the phone or on the computer much of the day. I decided to ask my boss about telecommuting from home one day a week. Her first answer was, "No, we've never done that and we don't want to set a bad precedent."

I had anticipated her response and had done my homework. I asked if she was willing to hear me out, and she said, "Sure." (She's actually a great boss.)

I laid out my plan in detail, including how we could work together to solve any problems that surfaced. I shared some research (from the Web) about telecommuters. That led to my list of expected benefits to her and to the team.

That all happened two years ago, and I've been telecommuting one day a week ever since. We've worked out all the glitches, and everyone is happy, especially me.

You guessed it: that's an example of requesting—and get-ting—outer space. Here's one that illustrates inner space:

Our team leader had a definite, preferred way of doing things. Some people on my team didn't seem to mind what I viewed as micro-managing. I was thinking about asking for a move, but I loved my teammates and the work. So I decided to talk with the team leader to negotiate a different way of working together.

I told him I could be a more valuable contributor to his group if I had a little more latitude. I talked about the processes I would use and told him I'd make sure my work measured up to his standards. I also said I would like to check in with him once a week, instead of daily. That was it. It seemed like no big deal to me.

It was a big deal to him, though. He said he was used to having more input into how things are done and was worried that I might get off track without his daily supervision.

I asked him to try it for one month, and I guaranteed I would do what it takes to generate great results. It worked, for him and for me. He still micromanages some people, but he has given me the space I need.

Both stories had happy endings. But not all requests for space go so smoothly. Your boss might want to say yes but decide to say no. Why? Because *your* boss has to please *her* boss, be fair to your coworkers, meet (or exceed) all goals, and, in the meantime, play by the *rules.* So, think about it: Why would she say yes to your request?

WIIFM (What's in It for Me?) Possibilities

Put yourself in your boss's shoes for a moment and ask, "What's in it for me to say yes?" The list could include such things as these:

- This employee will be happy and most likely produce more and stay here longer.
- This change could open up new opportunities for others on the team. For example, someone else can use his office when he's gone, or someone else can step into his role or lead the meetings.
- The rest of the team will see me as open-minded, creative, and collaborative. Most people want to work for a boss like that.
- If she doesn't need as much supervision, I'm freed up to do other things.
- If he is more enthusiastic or more creative, he might invent new products, services, or processes that could benefit us.

If you can't think of the WIIFM for your boss (*and* the team *and* the organization), take the time to do some homework before you ask for space.

So, to get some space, **try this:**

- Be clear about what you want and why you want it—how will it benefit you or increase your job satisfaction or productivity.

- Do your job well. If you're a top performer, your boss and organization will want you to stay, and they'll be more likely to consider your request.
- Find the WIIFM for your boss, team, and organization. How will this change benefit them? Try to quantify the results:
    - I'll have two extra hours to work, since I won't be commuting that day.
    - I'll be more creative with the new independence. You'll see a 50 percent increase in new ideas from me.
    - My loyalty, gratitude, and commitment will increase, because you were respectful enough to hear and agree to my request. (OK, this one is hard to measure but is significant enough to mention.)

What about Pandora's Box?

Your space-related request could benefit others in the organization. Think about the first people who asked for flexible hours or job sharing or family leave. They paved the way for some of the workplace improvements you may now be enjoying.

Your boss, however, might fear opening "Pandora's Box."

> *My boss said, "If I let you leave early on Fridays to attend your son's soccer game, your coworkers will want the same privilege. Then what?" Good question.*

> *I said I would make sure my work was done before leaving Friday afternoon, even if it meant working late earlier in the week. I also agreed to collaborate with every coworker and to work some "trades." I would help them if they would help me. We worked it out—as a team.*

You can reduce your boss's fear by trying this:

- List every potential downside you can think of and create several possible solutions for each. Be ready to discuss (even sell) your ideas.
- Put yourself in your colleagues' shoes and think about their potential complaints. (Of course, they might applaud.)
- Collaborate with your colleagues (and your boss) to find solutions and workarounds.
- Offer to help others with their workplace requests. They'll be more apt to support yours.

Your boss worries about fairness. Help him find ways to grant your request, while being fair to your colleagues. Brainstorm creative solutions that will benefit *everyone* on the team, and you'll be more likely to get the space you seek.

Space-Friendly Already?

Is your organization already giving you some of the inner and outer space you need? For example, are you free to:

Seen in a T-shirt shop in Great Falls, MT.

- Design, create, or do your work in your own unique way?
- Develop relationships, build connections, or find mentors?
- Question the rules (even your boss's rules) without repercussion?
- Learn and grow in many ways?
- Seek out more exciting, challenging work in the organization?
- Suggest or try flexible work hours or telecommuting?
- Dress the way you want occasionally?
- Decorate your office with vacation or family photos?

Are you maximizing and enjoying those freedoms? Have you said thank you? You might be happier with your work if you do more of what you're already given the space to do.

***

Chances are, no one's going to come along to offer you more space. You have to ask for it. The results could be liberating!

TRUTH: It Hurts ... Or Does It?

Why is it that getting feedback at work can feel like going to the dentist? We avoid it, pretend everything is just fine, and don't get preventive check ups. The result can be painful—ever had a root canal? We know dozens of people who derailed (failed to achieve the success they or others thought possible), largely because they didn't know how people saw them.

You need regular, honest feedback from your boss, coworkers, customers, and friends. You need straight talk from them about your relative strengths and weaknesses. That honest input is critical to your development, your success, and, ultimately, your satisfaction at work.

Yet, many people complain about not getting enough feedback. They say, "We don't have formal reviews," or "I get almost no input, and when I do, it isn't specific." They wait for input and expect honesty. Don't wait for your boss, or others, to tell you the truth. *Go after it.*

Thanks for the Gift (Send Socks Next Time)

Did you ever consider truth telling as a gift? If you see it that way, it will be much easier to take—and to give.

> *At the performance review meeting, my boss suggested that I attend a management training institute this coming quarter. When I asked why, he said that some people complained that I "didn't play well with others." He said my teammates found me to be a bit pushy and arrogant, and that I seemed to disregard their ideas and input. I admit I was shocked.*
>
> *So I went to "charm school"—you know, one of those "in ten days we'll fix you" seminars. I was closed at first, but part of the process was to get honest, detailed feedback from my coworkers, my boss, my employees, and even a couple of customers. The information was gathered anonymously, so people felt free to tell the truth, without fear of retribution. The process is called 360-degree feedback, and boy, was it valuable (also a little painful).*
>
> *I changed some of my behaviors immediately, just based on that feedback. I'm still working on some of the harder-to-change habits. One of the most valuable lessons I learned was that I need to take the blinders off. I need to know how oth-*

ers see me. Then I can decide if, what, or when I want to change.

So the next time someone says, "Can I give you some feedback?" say sure, thanks. Then look for the gift in it.

A Process, Not an Event

When you're ready to get some feedback, here's what you can do:

What? Decide what you want feedback about. Is it a skill, your behavior, your reputation?

Who? Figure out who can, and will, give you the most valuable, balanced input.

Where and when? Set up a meeting just for this purpose. Pick an appropriate place (not the hallway), and allow enough time. Invite your feedback provider, and tell him what you're hoping for.

How? Prepare (even practice) asking for input, and then hold the meeting. In that meeting, ask questions like, "What's one thing I could do more of, less of, or continue doing, to be more effective?"

Thank the feedback provider in person, in a note, or with a voice mail. And what's the best way to show your thanks? *Act* on the feedback. Use it to spark a change you want to make. (Remember to ask people whether they've seen you change. Watch your reputation shift.)

Development is a process, not an event. You'll be seeking feedback forever (or at least until you're perfect). As you try out new behaviors and test new learning, you'll need to enlist people who are willing to serve as truth tellers, over and over again. It works like this:

- You try a new behavior in the meeting.
- Your feedback provider takes notes as you participate in a new way.
- Immediately after the meeting, you get feedback.
- Next meeting, you try a modified approach.
- Your feedback provider takes notes—and so on.

How Can I Grow?

Your boss may hesitate to give you the truth for fear of offending you or, worse, sending you out the door to the competition. So she tells you how great you're doing (you nailed every objective), thanks you for your efforts this year, and excuses you until the next performance appraisal.

Terrific. You've arrived. You have nothing else to learn.

You know better. And if you're a solid performer, you actually *want to know* how you can improve. To get that kind of input from your boss, *ask* specific questions like these:

- If I aspire to move up in this organization, what skills do I need to strengthen?
- What one or two things should I do less of, in order to increase my effectiveness?

- If I were operating at a "10" on a 1—10 scale (10 being best), what would I be doing differently?

Imagine what you can do with *this* information!

Perception Is Reality

They're wrong. I'm not like that at all.

—Common lament of 360-degree feedback recipients

What's the buzz about you? Quiz yourself first. Are you seen as:

Intelligent, dedicated, hardworking? (Yes/No)
Very creative? (Yes/No)
The life of the party? (Yes/No)
Intimidating and hard to get along with? (Yes/No)

You get the idea.

Now interview a friend at work, someone who will tell you the truth. See how closely your reputation matches your self-perception.

Once you know how other people see you, you can choose one of these responses:

- Change. Replace behavior that doesn't work with behavior that does.
- Manage perceptions better. If they see you as uncaring and that's not really true, for example, *show* your caring side more. Over time your reputation will shift. (Be sure to ask others whether they see you changing.)
- Do nothing. But at least now you know.

You know yourself better than anyone else. You know your heart, your intentions, your values. You know whether another's perception of you is off-base. So take in the data and use it for your good and your growth. And, be sure to look for the *grain of truth* in the feedback.

> *I was told that I hogged the conversation, that no one else ever had a chance to talk when I was around. Talk about an exaggeration! I took note, though, and noticed on our next lunch outing that I was talking more than others—at least by a little bit.*

It's normal to get defensive when you receive tough feedback. Almost everyone does. Sometimes you even need to speak up for yourself, explain what you know to be true. But what if you believe the feedback you're getting is biased, inaccurate, or exaggerated? If you look closely enough, you might be able to find one grain of truth in it. Then ask, "What would happen if I changed that, by even a little?"

If one person calls you a horse, don't worry.

If two people call you a horse, start thinking about it.

If three people call you a horse, buy a saddle.

Tell It, Too

Seen at Quincy Market, Boston, MA.

What if a colleague, an employee, or your boss asks you for the truth? Ask first, to be sure they want praise and corrective (developmental) input. If they do, think of it as a gift and give it.

Your boss would probably like some feedback, too. Have you told him lately that

- He manages you well?
- He gave you an insight?
- His coaching is valuable?

***

If you've ever learned a new sport or taken music or dance lessons, you'll remember your coach giving you balanced feedback (praise and correction). You wanted honest input, and you accepted it as key to your success.

You need the truth to know where you stand and how you can succeed. Ask for it, see it as a gift, and then use it.

UNDERSTAND: Are You Listening Enough?

Most people need a reason to improve their listening skills (in fact, any skills). Here's a reason: You can get more of what you want from your work if you improve your listening (in meetings, at lunch, around the water cooler) and your *understanding* of:

- *How work really gets done.* Who are the *informal* leaders and what are the unwritten rules and accepted practices?
- *The challenges the organization faces.* Is the organization growing or downsizing?
  Pressured by Wall Street every quarter?
- *Changes coming.* Is there a new company direction, product line, or important customer?
- *The challenges your boss faces.* Is he or she understaffed, budget crunched, or pressured from above? It seems few employees stop to ask and then really try to understand what's going on with the boss.

When you know the answers to these questions and others, you can support your leaders better and become an even more valued resource to the organization. Once you're viewed that way, it's amazing how others will *help you* get more of what you want.

> *I couldn't believe I was promoted to this new role. I don't fit the stereotypical profile of the charismatic, outgoing, extroverted leader. In fact, I'm the opposite. My boss said that I am one of the most trusted, respected managers in the plant. He said that peers and employees see me as em-pathetic and are willing to confide in me. They bring me their ideas and even the bad news when things aren't going well. I know I'm a pretty good listener, but I never thought that skill could help get me promoted.*

Have *you* ever been accused of being a less-than-wonderful listener? If so, why is that? What are you thinking about, when you could be listening?

- I already know the punch line. I'm five steps ahead.
- I'm too busy for this. I have a stack of work on my desk.
- He's getting emotional. I'm checking out.
- What should my response be? How can I defend my position?
- She's so boring. I wonder what we should do for dinner.

How many ring true for you? ('Fess up.)

You might believe that it is great time management to have your mind busy while another person talks. Or to be planning your response so that you are ready the second the person stops speaking.

> *I admit it. I thought it was great "multitasking" to answer my e-mail while people talked to me. Now I realize the message I sent was, "You're not important." That's not the message I want to send. Now I turn off the e-mail, move work aside, and focus on the person in front of me.*

You might believe that your time and ideas are worth more than someone else's.

Or you may have just forgotten how to really focus on a person and listen deeply. Regardless of your reason, the result is the same: When you *tune out,* you *miss out.* You miss out on information. More important, you miss out on having a respectful relationship.

> ***If I want your opinion, I'll ask you to fill out the necessary forms.***
>
> —Anonymous

Listening experts talk about two levels of listening:

- Superficial listening (tuning in and out)
- Deep listening (focused on the speaker, honestly curious, which leads to understanding of the person)

Most of us spend little time in deep listening and aren't sure how to develop that skill. Here is one way.

Follow the Blinking Word

You're busy, maybe even overwhelmed. How can you quickly, easily, become a better listener? Try using a technique called *follow the blinking word.* Here is how it works.

Scenario: You're having lunch with Brad, a coworker. As he talks, you *decide* to get curious and *really listen.* Brad says, "This project is a nightmare. I can't wait for it to end."

1. Identify one word that *blinks* (stands out).

   "This project is a nightmare. I can't wait for it to end." You could inquire about project, nightmare, or end.

2. Ask about any one of the blinking words.

   "Tell me more about the work. What makes it a nightmare?"

3. Listen for Brad's answer.

   *"It's a nightmare because of the **cus-tomer."***

4. Notice the blinking words in his answer and question one of them.

   "What about the customer makes this so hard for you?"

5. Pay attention to Brad's answer.

   *"He **complains** about everything. Then he sets another **impossible deadline."***

6. Identify one blinking word in his answer and question it.

   "Does he have total control over your deadlines?" or "'Tell me about his biggest complaints."

See what we mean? If you focus on and get curious about one particular word, you learn a whole lot. And you can't make a mistake with the blinking word technique. If you followed the "wrong" word, the other person will correct you by elaborating on what he really meant.

Use questions that begin with such words or phrases as *how, why, where, when,* or *tell me about.* By following the blinking word, you go deeper into Brad's problem or story. He feels heard and believes you care enough to listen and maybe even help.

You'll notice that you can't tune in and out and still follow the blinking word.

(Do try this at home. Your spouse, kids, and friends will be pleasantly surprised at what a good listener you have become.)

Although the tongue weighs very little, few people are able to hold it.

—Anonymous

Listening leads to a better understanding of your environment (the organization, people, challenges, goals). And that understanding is key to having:

- Better relationships and more committed, loyal teammates, customers, and employees.
- More ideas and information (others *want* to share it).
- A boss who helps you get what you really want.

***

Listening beats talking. It may be counterintuitive to think that great listeners (not great talkers) get more of what they want in the workplace, but the evidence is conclusive. Organizations now hire, develop, and promote people who have not only IQ but *emotional intelligence* (EI, also called EQ). And key characteristics of emotionally intelligent people are their abilities to listen, empathize, and truly understand others. So tune in. Listen more.

Seen on an airplane heading east.

VALUES: What Matters Most?

For the past twenty years we've asked people of all ages, and from diverse industries, backgrounds, and occupations about their work-related values. Here is some of what we've heard:

I value—

- *The people I work with. I can't imagine not seeing them every day.*
- *This amazingly creative, challenging work. It stretches my brain and I love that.*
- *The chance to learn new things. That's key to me.*
- *A great boss who gives me freedom to do my work the way I want to do it.*

Values serve as filters for your decisions. They define what matters most to you. They are your personal bottom line. Values are so important that countless people make decisions to stay or go based on them. When your values match your work and your workplace, you feel "in sync." You have a sense of well-being. Your work feels meaningful, purposeful, and important.

And when your values are not met in your work and workplace, the opposite is true. Something is missing. And often, money or prestige doesn't compensate. Some people *do* stay but pay the price, emotionally, mentally, and even physically.

> ***Values are the emotional salary of work, and some folks are drawing no wages at all.***
>
> —Howard Figler, career consultant

If Howard's quote speaks to you, then take some time to consider the "emotional salary" you want and how to get it. Don't wait for your boss to notice that you seem unhappy. Don't wait for your organization to change. Get clear about what's unacceptable. Find a way to better align your values with the people, the workplace, or the work itself.

Define Your Values

Did you know that you probably spend at least two thousand hours a year working? You spend more time working than doing anything else, including sleeping. Clearly, it would be most satisfying to spend that time doing something you care about, something that matches your *values.*

To clarify your values, ask a friend to interview you—then you'll hear your own words—using these questions. As you answer each question, have your friend ask you *"Why?"*

- What would you miss most if you left this job or company?
- What made your "best job ever" your best job ever?
- When was a time you felt really energized here?
- What value would you not compromise, no matter what the consequence?

Your answers (and a good listener at the other end) will tell you a lot about your values.

> *I left my job at a large health benefits company to go to an insurance firm because the level of autonomy seemed so appealing—being responsible for my own success and tackling new accounts with my own creativity. Within months, I was miserable and didn't know why. When I had lunch with one of my former colleagues, she said she wasn't surprised at all. "You spent all your time here interacting with your colleagues, even when it wasn't totally necessary. You're a people person when it comes to the workplace." She was right. I thought I valued autonomy, and I do. But not at the expense of working relationships.*

Now compare your answers (to the questions above) with the values grid that follows on the next page. Which values would you prefer more of in your work life? Remember, values do change—especially in terms of *relative* importance. At work, for example, "opportunity for advancement" may be a top value at one point in your career, but it might be replaced later by "opportunity for personal creativity." Or, you might recognize that you truly do love the current work and that moving up (and away from it) is less important.

Check the seven values that are most important to you. Then make a check in the "want more" box, if that value is *not* currently being met to a high degree at work.

What did you learn from the grid? Do your values align with your work? For example, you may value making your own decisions, and you may be in an organization (or working for a boss) where values include structure, hierarchy, and rules. If there is a conflict, you'll want to think about its source. Is it with the work you're doing? Your boss? The team or organization in which you work? Before you can get more of what you want, evaluate the problem down to its source.

My Value	High Importance	Want More
Advancement		
Authority		
Autonomy		
Challenge		
Colleague interface		
Creativity		
Economic reward		
Fun		
Great leadership		
Helping others		

My Value	High Importance	Want More
High-integrity workplace		
Intellectual stimulation		
Learning		
Making decisions		
Performance feedback		
Prestige		
Recognition, respect		
Responsibility		
Routine		
Social responsibility		
Stability		
Structure		
Task variety		
Teamwork		
Technical competence		
Travel		
Work–life balance		
(Add one)		
(Add one)		
(Add one)		

Define Their Values

What does your boss, team, or organization value most? How do you know? To clearly define their values, you'll need to begin some serious exploration.

To identify your boss's values:

- Watch her closely. Actions speak louder than words.

  She said she valued work-life balance, yet she worked late every night and came in on the weekends.

- Notice when and what he praises and rewards (with you and others).

  He said he really appreciated my efforts to always come in on time. I notice he mentions how important that is to him in staff meetings, too.

- Ask her to help you in your exploration by looking at your values grid and talking about where her values and yours might be aligned and where they might be different. (She doesn't need to fill in the grid—a discussion will suffice.) Explain that you are seeking ways to improve your own satisfaction level at your current job.

To identify your team's values:

- Suggest that your work team talk about their values. Ask such questions as these:
  - What are our values as a team? How are they similar to and different from our values as individuals?
  - How do our differences improve the team's productivity? How do our differences get in the way?

- What can we learn, and what do we gain, from those with values different from our own?

- Note the behaviors, attitudes, and activities that your teammates support.
- Note also those they discourage.

To identify your organization's values:

- Learn the real but often unspoken cultural characteristics. We know some that are proud of a "burn 'em up" (opposite of work/life balance) culture. Others value creativity above all else. Others promote and support fun as a key organizational value.
- Check out policy and procedure manuals. Look for phrases like "We reward for performance" and "Employees are number one." Does this match your experience?
- Observe the preferences and behaviors of top leaders and other influential individuals. Who and what gets rewarded (or not)? Is the behavior consistent with published value statements (the one hanging on the wall)?
- Chat with people in the organization who have the long view of how values have changed over time. Identify why they have changed.

As you explore others' values, notice not just the differences but also the similarities. The differences you feel may be smaller than you thought. And some apparent differences in values may be just differences in style.

Now, Put It All Together

Once you know *your* values and are pretty sure about *theirs,* you can then try to align them. For example, if *fun at work* is a key value for you and you're working in a *fun-free zone,* see what you can do to bring some fun to the workplace. Talk to your manager and enlist his help (assuming he's not the "fun squelcher"). Good managers want you to be fully engaged and satisfied with your work. They know that means aligning the work and workplace to your key values.

> *We switched to a "profit center" approach that pitted account managers against each other. Top management was very excited about this. They provided training and gave pep talks. I hated it immediately and realized that I valued teamwork, not competition. I felt I had no choice but to dust off my resume. Then, by chance, I found that many other account managers were ready to bolt for the same reason. No one in our group enjoyed a highly competitive environment.*
>
> *So we went to our boss and told him exactly how we felt. He helped us see that the issue wasn't that the organization valued competition when employees did not. Instead, the company valued profit and thought this was a good way to get there. We came up with a plan for group profit centers, where teamwork rather than*

competition gets us to the goal. This approach works better for us, and top management is thrilled with our results.

If your boss says, "I don't know how to help," ask him, and/or others, to brainstorm possibilities with you. Often, the impossible becomes possible if you widen your search for solutions. And, if the fit doesn't look like it will get any better, you could look elsewhere *within* your organization. The culture, norms, and values can vary dramatically in different parts of the same organization.

Not everything that can be counted counts, and not everything that counts can be counted.

—Albert Einstein

***

Be vigilant about your values and notice how they align (or don't) with your work and your workplace. Remember that values sometimes change over time and that the values of others may change as well. Never give up seeking ways to fine-tune your values connection. It's your way of ensuring satisfaction from those two thousand hours (at least) that you annually put into your work.

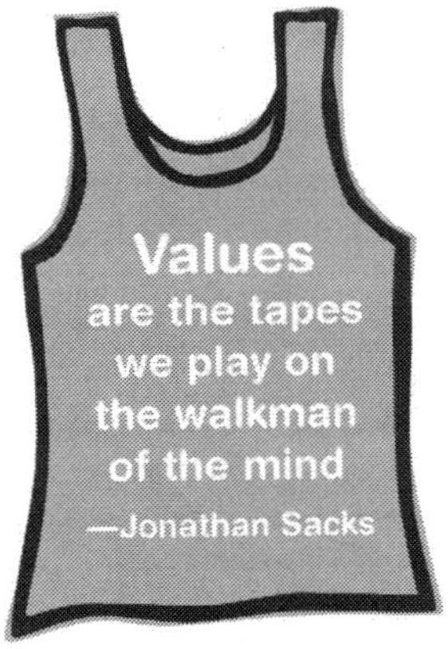

Seen at a car wash in Portland, OR.

WELLNESS: Time for a Checkup?

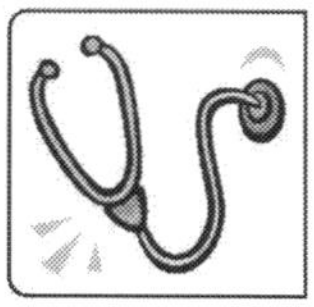

You know it. They know it. When you're feeling sick, overwhelmed, stressed out, or burned out, you are *not* performing at your best. And you're not enjoying your work as much as you could, either. Unfortunately, work—especially work you love—has a way of becoming the thousand-pound gorilla that pushes aside other pursuits.

> *I had been working seven days a week, fourteen-hour days for months—just to stay on top of my workload. I couldn't concentrate on anything for more than a few minutes at a time, and my creative juices had slowed to a trickle. I wasted time going for "wake-up" breaks and the tenth cup of coffee. That time could have been spent with my dog or on my bike. I had headaches and insomnia (when I took time to sleep!). That was a couple of years ago. I learned from that experience that my health is ultimately my responsibility. It doesn't mean I'm not committed to my work. I'll definitely put in the all-nighter occasionally, but I also make time for exercise, a*

social life, and some sleep. Guess what I found in the process? The time I take away from my work makes my time at work all the more productive.

It may be time for a checkup—literally, with your physician. Or, in this case, figuratively—conducted by you. Ask yourself, "Who or what causes your overload?" Sometimes it's you. How are you at managing your time, setting boundaries, or knowing when to say no? Are you clear about your priorities?

Sometimes, though, the overload is caused by *them.* Have *they* just merged, downsized, right-sized, grown by double (or even triple) digits, or handed you the work of three people?

Often it's both. But regardless of the cause, the result is the same. "Stop for lunch and you *are* lunch" is a quote we saw hanging on a wall in a Silicon Valley company. The message is harsh. Exhausted faces show the result. Talented workers often sacrifice health and well-being as they strive to satisfy deadlines, bottom lines, their own work ethic, and the boss. Ironically, it backfires. They *and* their work suffer.

People who cannot find time for recreation are obliged sooner or later to find time for illness.

—John Wanamaker

Here are some telltale signs of overload:

- Family members complain that they rarely see you.
- Your "toys" (tennis racquet, golf clubs, novels, saxophones, garden shears) are gathering dust.
- Your "vacations" are usually just long weekends.
- You consistently take work home and work evenings or weekends.
- You consistently arrive at work early and leave late.
- You rarely meet friends or family for lunch.
- Your work demands have prompted you to drop a hobby or fail to use a health club membership.

There are, no doubt, things your boss and your organization can do to help you reduce stress and increase your level of wellness. When you identify a way for them to help, *ask* them for it.

When all is said and done, though, it's up to *you* to put a little more health, energy, and balance into your life and work. When you do that, you'll find that your work satisfaction and success increase dramatically.

Manage Your Time (OK, How?)

One way of looking at it:

- A week is 168 hours. If you sleep 8 hours a night (recommended for wellness), you have 112 hours left.
- If you work 50 of those waking hours (including your commute), you have 62 hours left.
- If you regularly stay late, bring work home, or work on weekends, you might only have 30 or 40

hours left—fewer if you mismanage your time with distractions, procrastination, or unnecessary tasks.

So, manage your time wisely at work so you can spend *all your time,* both at work and away from work, productively and satisfyingly.

> *I worked late almost every day and knew I could probably change that if I really wanted to. I took a time management class. It gave me great ideas and a bunch of new tools and techniques, guaranteed to give me more time to spend thinking, playing, and exercising. It also tipped me off to my biggest time zapper at work—my spontaneous chats with coworkers. I kept a log of how much time I spent when people wandered into my cubicle—or I wandered into theirs. It added up to a whopping hour a day on average! It's been tough, but I've managed to cut that in half (and still feel like I'm part of the social environment that I love). The thirty minutes saved provides me the latitude to spend the "found" time both reducing my ever-growing pile of work and leaving work earlier. I beat the rush hour and have more time with my family.*

What are you doing with the thirty-plus hours you have left, after sleeping and working? If you're a typical American, you're staring at some kind of screen (TV or computer) on average of five to six hours a day. That's thirty-five to forty-two hours per week. That leaves you with *zero* time to exercise, interact with your family, or indulge in a favorite hobby. No wonder people complain that they have no time! If you turned off the television and computer just two days a week, think what you could do for your health and well-being.

Here's another way of running the numbers. If you live to your seventieth birthday, you will spend:

- twenty-three years of your life sleeping,
- seventeen years working,
- eleven years watching TV, and
- two years getting ready to go.

What if you spent just a few of those years doing something else?

To maintain your health or *get* healthy, you sometimes have to say no to a good idea. You have to know when to draw the line.

> *I was asked to chair a committee for this great cause I believe in. I'm proud I had the courage to say no. It was hard to do, but I know the limits of my time and my priorities. I'd learned the hard way.*

Sleep and Eat (Duh!)

Not such a novel idea. Yet talented people forget to do just this.

> *I was proud of my ability to live on coffee, Krispy Kremes, and four hours of sleep a night—proud until my overdue physical checkup showed I was forty pounds overweight and borderline diabetic. I talked it over with my boss and asked for his support (even stern reminders) for*

a whole new way of working—and living. Now I sleep more, take a real lunch break, eat real food, and exercise after work. I feel better, and my productivity has actually gone up.

What are you eating, and how much are you sleeping (yes, counting the naps at your desk)? How can you change? When will you start? Whom will you tell and enroll to assist you in your efforts?

Exercise (Groan)

Does it really have to hurt to qualify as exercise?

The phrase "no pain, no gain" only works for a small percentage of people (triathletes and body-builders come to mind). Most sensible human beings actually spend their lives trying to avoid pain.

I've joined the gym at least a dozen times. I go for a while, just until my muscles stop hurting so much—and then I start finding reasons to skip a workout (my cat had his teeth cleaned, the car needs washing, etc.) Finally I quit. Then I join again on January 4.

The gym may be your thing. If so, go for it! But don't feel bad if it just isn't you. The key is to find exercise you actually enjoy. If you like it, you're much more likely to keep it up.

Seen in a gym in Cambria, CA.

I'd always found it hard to fit regular exercise into my busy schedule. I'm responsible for a large group of people, and there are never enough hours in the day. One day, a colleague with a similar job and similar responsibilities in another kind of organization invited me to meet for an early-morning walk. She had a work problem and wanted my advice. We walked for four miles before either of us even realized it. And we solved her problem as well as one of mine. Now it's a regular part of our work lives. We've been walking and talking at least once a week for seventeen years.

And maybe variety is the spice of life for you. If so, walk one day, garden the next, bungee jump the next.

Learn Stress Management and Relaxation (Ohhmm)

Stress is an ignorant state. It believes that everything is an emergency.

—Natalie Goldberg

Do you know how to breathe? *Really* breathe?

I went on a five-day team-building outing with my colleagues. Besides learning how to work more effectively together, we had outdoor activities and stress management sessions. That's where we learned to breathe, *relax our ever-busy minds, and focus on some beautiful vacation scene. We learned to stop negative thinking midstream and try some affirmation instead. My favorite new phrase when I'm feeling overwhelmed is, "It'll all get done—it always does." Sounds corny, but it actually works for me.*

Try these:

- The next time you feel stressed, find a quiet place (it might have to be the restroom). Breathe slowly and focus on nothing else but your breath going in and out of your lungs.
- Rent a relaxation CD or take a class. Find one technique that works for you.
- Create three custom affirmations (positive statements) that seem to help you.

> *My favorite affirmation makes me grin—and that makes me relax. It goes like this: "I love deadlines. I like the whooshing sound they make as they fly by."*

Unleash and Unplug (Ahhh)

The communication age is just great, isn't it? People can reach you anytime, anywhere, anyplace.

> *I suggested to my boss that we have a "leash-free" Friday morning, just to see what it might be like and see how much work we might get done. There were no buzzing beepers or chirping Blackberries. It worked so well that he's made it a new Friday morning standard. Not only did our stress levels go down on that one day a week, but our productivity soared.*

Have you considered:

- Taking a vacation? That means a time-out from work. No laptop, no cell phone, no beeper.
- Turning your blinking, buzzing, ringing communication tools off when you're having dinner with friends and family?
- Unplugging your brain from your work? See a movie, play a game, build something, play some music, take pictures, learn to draw, birdwatch, journal, fix a bike—in the middle of the week!

Baby Steps for Better Balance

Seen at a health food store in Ligonier, PA.

If you're out of balance and spending more time at work (or *doing* work) than you want, here are a few ideas. Start slowly—it could be a shock to your system!

- Do not go into the office on any weekend this month.
- Take work home only twice this week.
- Leave exactly on time at least once this week.
- Say no to the next after-hours meeting. (Gulp!)
- Leave the building for lunch every other day this week.
- Rejoin your health club.

***

You are ultimately in charge of your own state of health and well-being. Ask your boss and others for help in accomplishing your wellness

goals. But take control and *do something* now to increase your own level of mental, emotional, and physical fitness. Schedule that checkup so you don't check out! We're going for a walk now.

X-ERS AND OTHER GENRATIONS: Bridge the Gap

Have you ever:

- Wondered why he didn't "respect his elders"?
- Been irritated with her apparent "blind loyalty"?
- Felt angry because he expects you to be a "workaholic" like he is?
- Been frustrated by his preference for e-mail over telephone communication?

His e-mail communication is so rude. No salutation or punctuation and no capital letters at all. All I get are cryptic messages flying my way daily. I was taught to start and end letters properly, with a "Dear Joe" and a "thank you" and a "Sincerely, Mike." It's no wonder we don't get along very well.

Challenges like these can occur because of individual differences. And individual differences are often amplified by the generation gap. Some people become so frustrated or irritated with their younger or older colleagues that they disengage. They quit communicating or interacting. Some-times, if the conflict persists, they even consider leaving their workplaces.

Experts say that for the first time ever, there are four distinct generations in the workplace. The names and definitions of these groups vary, depending on whose research you read. One commonly accepted labeling is the Matures (those born 1933–1945), Boomers (1946–1964), Gen-X-ers (1965–1976), and Gen-Y's (1977–1994).

Social scientists have conducted hundreds of studies and written dozens of books on the topic of the generations and the gaps between them. Each generation brings its unique history, perspective, attitudes, values, behaviors, and set of expectations, shaped by the cultural influences of their era.

If you're experiencing generation gaps with colleagues, bosses, or employees, don't pull away and don't jump ship—at least not until after you've tried to bridge the gap. By "bridge the gap," we mean:

- Appreciate what was happening in the world as they grew up, the experiences that shaped their views of the world and of work.
- Learn from and empathize with them. See things from their perspectives.
- Build relationships or collaborations that work for you and them.

Don't wait for *them* to take the first steps toward bridging the gap. You go first. Why? Because they might not take the first step. Because you lose precious productive time while you wait for them to go first. Because in the process of bridging the gap, you'll gain satisfaction and new learning.

Gaps at Work

Blending the generations at work can be exciting and enriching at best, and irritating or frustrating at worst.

> *The leader of my project does not understand my needs and isn't trying to understand. I believe that the root problem is the big difference in our generational backgrounds. He's the new kid on the block, still out to prove his worth. I'm the seasoned veteran. We value different things, largely because we're at different stages of our careers, but partly because of the different ways we have grown up and have lived our lives. I'm considering taking my retirement early. It's the only viable option I seem to have. I never dreamed it would be this uncomfortable.*

If you've ever felt this way, take heart. There is a lot you can do to bridge the gap.

What's Your View?

If you have difficulty working with someone, or several people, a generation (or two) younger or older than you, it could be because of your assumptions or beliefs about that group of people. Maybe your assumptions are true—and maybe they're not.

Do you see younger colleagues, subordinates, or bosses as naïve, inexperienced, demanding kids? Or do you see:

- Refreshing energy and optimism?
- Quick, alert minds that could help you solve a problem?
- Cutting-edge skills and techniques?
- People thriving on challenge, learning, and ambitious goals?
- Fresh perspectives brought from other organizations, schools or countries?
- ______ What else?

> *His enthusiasm and unbridled optimism irritated me. He was so young. He knew nothing about this organization, the leaders, the real values of this place. I stayed out of his way and did my work—and I never offered to help.*
>
> *Then one day we started **talking** in the break room, and he asked about my history here. I started **telling stories** about our successes and failures, and about the founders and all the changes I'd seen. He **compared** the organization he last worked in to this one and listed the many ways that this organization is better. We **listened** to each other. That was four years ago, and, since then, we've become friends and colleagues. I've actually learned some optimism, and he knows a lot more about this organization.*

When you look at your older colleagues, subordinates, or bosses, do you see silver or gold? Do you view them as expensive, over the hill, burned out, obsolete, or change-resistant? Or are they:

- Valuable sources of organizational history?
- Sources of wisdom, perspective, experience, or patience?
- Great leaders?
- Models of commitment, loyalty, and dedication?
- Safe harbors of noncompetitive advice and counsel?
- ______ What else?

> *My boss is thirty years older than I am. At first the gap really bothered me. We were so different in our views. I want a life outside of work, and he sees that as being uncommitted to the job. I'm also very independent and don't do well with a controlling boss. We grew up in very different worlds and have very different expectations about work.*
>
> *One day I invited him to coffee to* ***talk about those different views.*** *I* ***learned*** *a lot about his background and why he sees things as he does. He learned from me, too. I guess that is the key to our good working relationship today. We're willing to talk about our differences and try to* ***understand*** *the other person's perspective. In many ways I actually benefit from the generation gap that irritated me initially.*

You'll notice that the "checked" lists earlier could also apply to people in the opposite category (young or old). You probably know older colleagues with *quick minds* and *cutting-edge skills.* And you know younger colleagues who are wonderful *leaders* and *wise* beyond their years. We need to test *all* of our assumptions as we strive to understand the people with whom we work. *Individual differences must always be taken into account!*

Gap Bridging

The clues to effectively bridging the gap were printed in **bold** in the stories you just read. If you find yourself frustrated or disengaged because of a generation misunderstanding or clash, consider any or all of these ideas:

- **Talk.** Take the lead. Go for coffee to talk about the gap. Describe how you feel, what you see. Explain your points of view. Stories are helpful, too. They can illustrate a perspective and describe how you came to feel or act the way you do. Tell stories about bosses (good and bad), work successes and failures, fears overcome, and opportunities missed. Be sure to give the other person a chance to tell stories, too!
- **Listen.** *Actively* listen. Ask, "How did that happen?" "Who was involved?" "How did that impact you?" Be truly interested in the answers. The more you listen, the more you'll learn. Compare your experiences and perspectives. How are they different (e.g., expectation of job security and stability)? How are they the same (e.g., need for reward and recognition)? How do those experiences impact your thinking today?

Seen at a fiftieth birthday party.

- **Understand.** Understand the cultural forces that shaped the other person. Who were the teachers, role models, and idols? What social, political, and technical challenges and changes influenced the experience (e.g., latch-key kids, the Cold War, the Great Depression, MTV, polio, computers, video games)? How were those experiences similar to or different from yours?
- **Learn.** What skills, traits, or behaviors could you learn? What could someone else teach you about work-life balance? Or about the latest computer technology? Are there leadership skills you could teach each other?

***

The generation gap may feel huge at times. Don't let it block effective, enjoyable relationships or cause you to lose enthusiasm for your work or your workplace. Take steps toward bridging the

gap. Talk it out. Explain yourself and seek to understand another point of view.

YIELD: Get Out of Your Own Way

Yielding is rare, in life and at work. That fact is painfully evident when trying to merge onto a busy highway. Many people believe they need to have control, win every battle, be first, and be right, to get what they want and need. Ironically, the opposite is true. Sometimes what serves you best is to get out of your own way and yield the right-of-way to someone else. To increase your satisfaction, personal growth, and energy at work, give yielding a try.

> *I'm used to being in control and acting independently. Once I figure out what I'm going to do and how I want to do it, I'm like a bullet train: Just try to stop me. A coworker on a major project suggested that we bring in several experts for a midpoint review, just to be sure we were on track.*
>
> *I balked, then said, "OK, if you really think we should." The review process was painful but absolutely crucial. After the review, we changed course so dramatically that it was al-*

most like starting over. The project is a roaring success. Thank goodness I yielded—that time.

How good are you at yielding? **Interview yourself:**

- How often do I pleasantly let the other person go first—at meetings or intersections, in lines, boarding an airplane?
- How often do I go with the other person's idea, even when it differs dramatically from mine?
- How often am I willing to back down, or even start over, once my course is set?

If you answered "never" to all three questions, you may have heard once or twice that you're pushy or overly controlling. Even if you answered "seldom" or "occasionally," you could probably benefit from some *yield lessons.*

Yield Lessons: Why and How to Yield

If you are a self-starter, a good performer, or driven by results, you may have the toughest time yielding. Your attitude could be

The question isn't who is going to let me—it's who is going to stop me.

If that sounds like you, consider yielding occasionally because:

- You can't *always* be right. Sometimes someone else has a better solution, updated information, or a fresh perspective.
- Others will be more cooperative when you give them a turn—a chance to create, to be in

charge, to speak up. When they cooperate, you'll be able to accomplish more.

- You'll get more positive press. Remember what people said about the last person who cut in line, monopolized the conversation, or refused to reconsider a faulty decision?
- You'll have more success. You've heard the saying "two heads are better than one." When you really *listen* to others' ideas, you'll notice your own creativity increases.

That's the *why* of yielding. Here's the *how.*

Slow Down—You Move Too Fast

To yield more effectively, practice slowing down.

Try this—next week:

- Let someone go ahead of you (at a meeting, in line, at the cafeteria, boarding a bus).
- The next time you're about to speak up first (again), *stop*—breathe—count to five. If you yield and no one says anything, it's your turn.
- Let go of ego, pride, stubbornness, or power long enough to hear and act on *one* idea, suggestion, or complaint from a coworker, employee, customer, or your boss. Ask yourself, "What if? What if we followed his suggestion, instead of my way? What's the downside compared to the upside?" If the risk is minimal, choose to go with his idea this time.

My coworkers and employees complained to my boss that I never accepted their ideas. They thought I was so in love with my own ideas that I shut theirs out. I was shocked. That was ten years ago. Since then, I've changed. I stop, listen to, and act on others' ideas. The truth is that often I notice they are even better than, or complement, mine.

How to Get Your Boss to Yield

If you have a boss who is accustomed to calling the shots, making the decisions, you may wonder how you'll get her to yield, if even just a little. First, make sure you're a solid performer. Nail your goals and prove yourself trustworthy.

Then, have a chat with her. Ask her for more independence, more creative freedom, or fewer checks and balances. Be as specific as you can. Give a concrete example of what independence would look like and where you might try it out in the next sixty days. The more specific you are, the more likely you'll be heard.

Explain how important this change is to you and describe what's in it for her. Most bosses will agree to try something that will lead to greater job satisfaction, better performance, and increased odds that you'll stick around.

Too Much of a Good Thing?

Can you yield too much? Any virtue can be a vice if you overdo it.

Overyield Checklist

Seen in a line at the movies.

Which of the following statements are true for you? You're yielding too much if:

- You never get to the front of the line.
- Your ideas never get heard, let alone adopted.
- You back down, start over, and then back down again—all in one day.

If you checked any of these, you might need to practice standing up for yourself, speaking your mind, or offering your ideas. Read "Ask" and "Buck" (well, maybe the whole book) to increase your confidence and your skill.

***

Picture busy highway on-ramps, intersections with no stop signs, and lines forming at the movies. How shocked are you when someone

says, "*You* go first"? When they do that, they are yielding the right-of-way to you.

It may seem counterintuitive but it's true. Yielding (a form of *giving)* will help you *get* more of what you want in the workplace.

ZENITH: Are We There Yet?

Zē-nith: the peak, the greatest height

My work was great. Every project, every new position in the organization seemed better than the last. Just as I thought it couldn't get any better, the unexpected happened. I became disenchanted with my work. Part of it was due to my having a new boss, with whom I didn't really connect. But there was more to it than that.

I questioned everything: What was missing? What did I really want? Could I get it here? I searched, too. I would not settle for "ho-hum" work, and I knew it was up to me to find what I wanted most.

My persistence paid off. I now have exciting, meaningful work and a boss I really enjoy. I know, though, that things will change again. It's up to me to keep reaching for that "happiest" state of being.

Our work lives sometimes feel like a constant climb, and just as we did when we were kids, we wonder how long it will take to "get there."

"Getting there" in this case represents true workplace satisfaction. For most of us, that level of satisfaction is fleeting. Once we arrive, we set new goals or strive for yet a higher level of achievement or learning or joy. That could feel frustrating, except for the fact that the journey itself can be exhilarating. Satisfaction often comes not just from reaching the peak but also in traveling to it.

Satisfaction Requires Action

No one but you can take responsibility for your workplace satisfaction. Yes, there are actions your manager can take, and yes, there are actions your organizational leaders can take, but in the end it's all up to you. You're in charge of finding and working toward the zenith.

We've provided twenty-six sets of ideas. And you undoubtedly thought of others while you read this book. Your satisfaction at work will depend on your willingness to follow through on some of those ideas. Here's one more chance to question yourself. Be honest. You're the only one who really knows how serious you are about taking action. Ready? Mark your responses right in this book.

Do you...	I do	I don't	I'm trying to
(Ask) Know what you want and ask for it?			
(Buck) Take full responsibility for your workplace satisfaction and success?			
(Career) Manage your own career?			

Do you…	I do	I don't	I'm trying to
(Dignity) Get the respect you want in your work-place?			
(Enrich) Keep your current job interesting?			
(Family) Balance the time you spend at work and with your family?			
(Goals) Pursue several different career options?			
(Hire) Learn the ropes in any new job and market yourself internally?			
(Information) Search for plenty of information about your workplace?			
(Jerk) Deal effectively with jerks at work?			
(Kicks) Have more fun, right where you are?			
(Link) Connect to others in your workplace?			
(Mentor) Find the mentors you need?			
(Numbers) Know how to get paid what you're worth?			
(Opportunities) Seek, see, and seize opportunities at work?			
(Passion) Build passion into your work?			
(Question) Question the rules when they don't make sense?			

Do you...	I do	I don't	I'm trying to
(Reward) Look for reward in your work?			
(Space) Request the elbow room you need?			
(Truth) Solicit feedback to know how others see you?			
(Understand) Listen hard to understand others?			
(Values) Determine what you value and how to find it on the job?			
(Wellness) Take great care of yourself?			
(X-ers and Other Generations) Bridge the generation gaps at work?			
(Yield) Give the "right of way" to others to get results?			
(Zenith) Continually strive for higher levels of workplace satisfaction?			

Are you willing to reread a chapter or two? Take a few more actions? Let this checklist guide you.

If you've been at your current workplace six months or more, you already have created at least some equity (social, skill, influence, financial). It makes sense to build on that equity however you can. And when things change (they always do), you may need to shift your attitude and approach. Different chapters in the book will move to the "front burner." Consider what new actions might make sense before you even *think about* moving to the last chapter.

***

You deserve to have meaningful work. We all do. This book challenges you *not* to settle for less and *not* to search immediately for satisfaction elsewhere. You don't have to take what you get, so go get what you want. Look for it where you are first. It could be there.

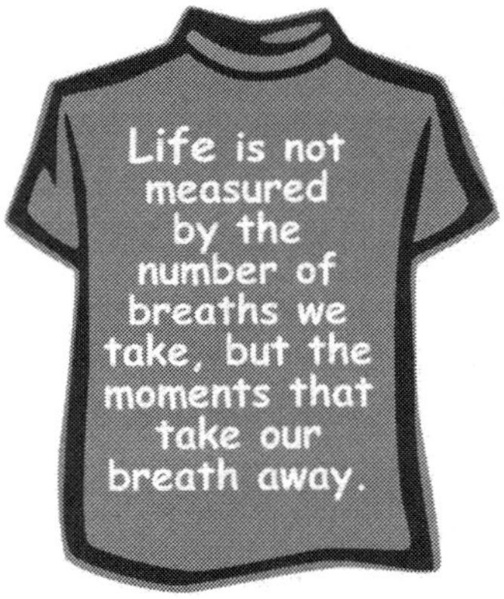

Seen in Stanley Park, Vancouver, British Columbia.

IF BUT IF YOU MUST LEAVE

So, you still think you have to go. You tried everything *(really)*, A through Z, and cannot get more of what you want where you are.

Apply the brakes. Don't make a move until you can clearly state what you're going after, and you've investigated the new opportunity thoroughly. If you must go, be certain you're leaving for something better.

> *I was so unhappy in my job. I merely existed for two years. Finally I decided to bite the bullet and leave. I immediately started my search. I was amazed to find something quickly. It seemed perfect. Well, I have been here almost a year... and you know, this job has some of the same problems my last job did, and some new ones. I guess it wasn't so perfect after all.*

Analyze This

If you've read this book and answered its questions, you may know what you're looking for next, inside or outside your organization. It's vital that you're clear about:

- The kind of work you want to do next.

- The kind of boss, team, or work environment you are seeking.
- The things that matter most to you. Is it the money? The creativity or challenge of the work? The chance to learn something new?

Can you clearly state your wants and needs now? If so, you're ready to investigate the next opportunity and increase your odds of making a great choice.

> *I asked five friends whether I should accept a job offer. They all said, "Jump at it. It's better money." I thought more about it and decided to stay right where I am. It turns out that money is just one factor among many that matter to me. I also want independence and a highly creative workplace. When I analyzed my goals and then asked more questions, I realized the new, exciting opportunity doesn't measure up to the one I have.*

Review your equity. What have you invested in your current job or workplace? How soon (if ever) will you be able to recover your investments? **Interview yourself:**

- *Skill equity:* Do I have skills that are highly respected here? Have I proven my expertise? How long will it take to build that reputation and respect in the next workplace?
- *Social equity:* How important are my relationships here? How difficult will it be to develop equivalent friendships, collaborations, and customer connections?

- *Influence equity:* Can I strongly impact decisions and get necessary resources here? How easy is it for me to move my ideas through the system? How long will it take to build that kind of power elsewhere?
- *Financial equity:* How much money will I leave behind, given my retirement plan, investments, current salary, bonus, and insurance?

Investigate That

If you're seriously considering a move to a different organization, or there's a hot offer on the table, become a super-sleuth. Try some of these techniques to help you make a sound decision:

- Ask whether you can talk with future teammates. Ask them about the work, the boss, the people, the culture, and the future. Watch their body language as you ask questions and read between the lines. Do they love their work? The organization?
- Hang out in the parking lot of the new organization early in the morning, at quitting time, or later at night. How many people arrive at daybreak and stay until midnight? How empty is the parking lot at 5P.M.? 10P.M.? How thrilled, exhausted, vibrant, trampled do they look as they arrive? As they leave?
- If there's a company lunchroom that's open to the public, have lunch there. Eavesdrop. What are employees talking about? How does it feel? (How's the food?)

- Find someone in a competitor's organization who will chat with you about your potential new employer. What do they think of the organization? What are its strengths? Weaknesses? Find vendors, customers, and former employees and ask them the same questions.
- Use the Internet. If the potential employer is a publicly held company, download its annual report, and, if necessary, get help interpreting it. Go to nontraditional sites too, such as www.vault.com, where dissatisfied employees go to vent. (Wall Street checks these sites regularly!)

Going Out on Your Own?

If you are considering starting your own business rather than working for someone else, you'll still need to investigate and ask great questions of others and of yourself. Before you hang your own shingle, here is some additional detective work you can do:

- Talk to others who have started businesses. Ask what they like best and least about running their own show. What would they do differently if they were to start over?
- Create a business plan and have several people familiar with plans of this nature read it, question you, and help you improve it.
- **Interview yourself:**
    - Am I a *self-starter?* Disciplined?
    - Do I enjoy working alone much of the time?
    - Am I OK with ambiguity and uncertainty?

- Is it OK not to have a regular stream of income?
- Will I like marketing myself and my business?

Too many people start their own businesses because they're fed up or burned out. Starting and running your own business has its own set of risks and rewards. Do your homework before taking this route.

Before you go, take one more look at your needs and wants. Reconsider the equity question. Glance through this book again and try out one more strategy. Or run your ideas by one more person. You might find what you're looking for right where you are. (Well, we thought it was worth a try.)

Go for It

Seen at a recruiting conference, Kansas City, MO.

But, if you must go, do so with your eyes wide open. When opportunity knocks with a *perfect job* in a *perfect location* with a perfect boss, be ready. Know what you want, and then launch an investigation.

Don't go until you *know* you're going to greener grass. And when you get there, use this book again. If you've marked it up, all the better. It's now your guidebook to getting more of what you want, *wherever you are.*

ABOUT THE AUTHORS

The authors of this book were introduced to each other by a mutual friend who insisted that they had a great deal in common, both personally and professionally. She was right on both counts. (Thank you, Susan!)

Their professional partnership produced their first book, *Love 'Em or Lose 'Em: Getting Good People to Stay,* and a host of workshops and products to support managers in their efforts to engage and retain their talent. Their continued work together led to many discussions and debates and eventually gave way to the book that is now in your hands.

Authors Sharon Jordan-Evans and Beverly Kaye

Their friendship enables them to support one another in the process of growing their individual businesses and growing their families as well.

Bev is the founder and CEO of Career Systems International, a training, consulting, and product development company specializing in talent management. She is also the author of the career development classic, *Up Is Not the Only Way.* She received her doctorate from UCLA. Bev lives in Sherman Oaks with her husband Barry (a newly retired "rocket scientist"), their teenage daughter Lindsey, and Roxy (part Dalmatian, part terrier—if you can imagine that!).

Sharon lives about four hours north of Bev, in Cambria, California. She is the president of her own consulting organization, The Jordan Evans Group, which specializes in executive coaching, leadership development, and retention and engagement. Sharon received her master's degree in organization development from Central Washington University. She lives with her husband Mike (a retired aeronautical engineer turned designer/builder), and Oreo, her Shih Tzu puppy. She has four grown children—Shelby, Travis, Matt, and Kellie—and two grandchildren. All (luckily) live on the West Coast.

Bev and Sharon can be spotted on long beach walks (La-guna or Moonstone), exercising Roxy and Oreo, or brain-storming their next creative idea in a coffee shop—anywhere.

WORKING WITH THE AUTHORS

Bev and Sharon enjoy delivering joint keynote speeches and partnering on their organizational consulting services. In addition, they each have their own companies that operate independently and offer an array of specialized services. You can learn more about them by visiting their individual Web sites or their joint Web site:

www.LoveItDontLeaveIt.com

Career Systems International (CSI), a Beverly Kaye Company

CSI is a consulting, training, and product-driven organization focusing on talent management solutions. It is committed to providing innovative, user-friendly, and practical state-of-the-art solutions in the areas of engagement, retention, career development, and mentoring. Its award-winning offerings include self-assessment tools, instructor-led and Web-enabled workshops, and instruments. Generic and customized approaches are available. All CSI materials are designed to be deceptively simple, delightfully engaging, and deliberately flexible.

Contact Information

Career Systems International

www.CareerSystemsIntl.com
900 James Avenue
Scranton, PA 18510
Phone: (800)577-6916
Fax: (570)346-8606

The Jordan Evans Group

The Jordan Evans Group is a leadership consulting firm dedicated to increasing employee engagement, effectiveness, and retention. Sharon Jordan-Evans, president, is a prominent workplace consultant, a certified executive coach, and a keynote speaker, working with organizations throughout North America, Europe, and Australia. Her clients represent virtually all industries and many Fortune 500 companies such as Boeing, Southwest Airlines, LSI Logic, and Universal Studios.

Contact Information

The Jordan Evans Group
www.jeg.org
565 Chiswick Way
Cambria, CA 93428
Phone: (805)927-1432
Fax: (805)927-7756

GOING DEEPER: Individual & Organizational Love It Resources

If you found the tips and tools in this book useful, you may want to explore some of the resources listed below.

INDIVIDUAL TOOLS

(Available in print and on the internet)

Career: *The Career Action Inventory*™ covers the five critical steps in the development process, assesses the actions you've taken so far in your career and provides you with steps to optimize your career plan.

Goals: *The Career Leverage Inventory*™ is an assessment to determine your individual preference for six different career path options. Results are measured and prioritized using a series of reality-testing questions.

Link: *The Connections Map*™ provides step-by-step instructions for building a network within your organization.

Passion: *The Creative Mind Profile™* identifies your creative style, and suggests actions for working with others.

Truth: *The Feedback Wheel™* provides tips for effectively giving and receiving feedback.

Values: *The Invest in your Values™ Instrument* helps prioritize your values, determine the degree each is realized in your job, and then design the steps needed to best achieve them.

X'rs and Others: *The Generation Time Line* improves your effectiveness in interacting with associates from all generations by helping understand the issues and events surrounding each of the four generations in the workforce.

WORKSHOP

SatisfACTION Power™ is a half-day workshop containing a unique peer-coaching element bringing alive the ideas in the book, and starts the process of blueprinting individual satisfaction plans.

E LEARNING

Just Ask is an online tool that turns common dissatisfiers into concrete actions that employees can pursue on their own behalf. Suggestions and tips go beyond those described in the book.

INTERNET PORTAL FOR WORK SATISFACTION

The *Love It Club*™ offers the best of the best work satisfaction resources in a fascinating and fun experience. Users get exactly what they want—exactly when they need it. Available to individual consumers and through organization-wide enrollment.

Information on all of these resources as well as other learning aides can be found at:

www.careersystemsintl.com
www.loveitdontleaveit.com

And for those who manage others...

Love 'Em or Lose 'Em

Getting Good People to Stay
Beverly Kaye and Sharon Jordan-Evans

Regardless of economic swings or unemployment statistics, you need your stars to stay. And you need them not just to stay, but also to be engaged, motivated and producing at their peak. This revised and updated edition offers 26 strategies, from A to Z—that managers can use to address their concerns and keep them on the team.

Retention and Engagement Workshop

Love 'Em or Lose 'Em: Building Loyalty and Commitment in the Workplace: A flexible workshop (available online and facilitator-led) that helps managers identify talent risks, build skills and behaviors, increase engagement, and develop individualized engagement and retention plans.

Love 'Em Coupons

26 coupons managers can give to employees to implement specific A-to-Z strategies.

Love 'Em ThinkPak/A-Z Card Sort

Guides users in identifying the engagement climate at an organizational, departmental or team level.

Retention Deficit Disorder

Helps managers recognize behaviors that drive talent away, and then map out their own recovery plan.

Retention-Focused Manager

A 180° survey for managers and their staff to identify and rate the impact of various managerial behaviors on employee retention and engagement.

To order, or to obtain more information about these and other tools, call Career Systems International at (800)577-6916 or email us at HQ@csibka.com

Berrett-Koehler Publishers

Berrett-Koehler is an independent publisher of books and other publications at the leading edge of new thinking and innovative practice on work, business, management, leadership, stewardship, career development, human resources, entrepreneurship, and global sustainability.

Since the company's founding in 1992, we have been committed to creating a world that works for all by publishing books that help us to integrate our values with our work and work lives, and to create more humane and effective organizations.

We have chosen to focus on the areas of work, business, and organizations, because these are central elements in many people's lives today. Furthermore, the work world is going through tumultuous changes, from the decline of job security to the rise of new structures for organizing people and work. We believe that change is needed at all levels—individual, organizational, community, and global—and our publications address each of these levels.

To find out about our new books,
special offers,
free excerpts,
and much more,
subscribe to our free monthly eNewsletter at

www.bkconnection.com

More books from Berrett-Koehler Publishers

Repacking Your Bags

Lighten Your Load for the Rest of Your Life 2nd Edition
Richard J. Leider and David A. Shapiro

Learn how to climb out from under the many burdens you're carrying and find the fulfillment that's missing in your life. A simple yet elegant process teaches you to balance the demands of work, love, and place in order to create and live your own vision of success.

Getting Things Done When You Are Not In Charge

2nd Edition
Geoffrey M. Bellman

Geoff Bellman offers practical guidance for all of us who are not in charge on how to make a difference in our organizations and accomplish our own goals while supporting the work of others. This new edition of the international bestseller has been streamlined and thoroughly updated with new material.

The Blind Men and the Elephant

Mastering Project Work
David A. Schmaltz

In this book Schmaltz identifies the most common root cause of project failure: incoherence. He provides a set of simple techniques that anyone can use to encourage project coherence and transform their "wicked project fuzziness" into personally meaningful results. This book explores just how much influence you command and undermines the most common excuses that keep people trapped in meaningless pursuits.

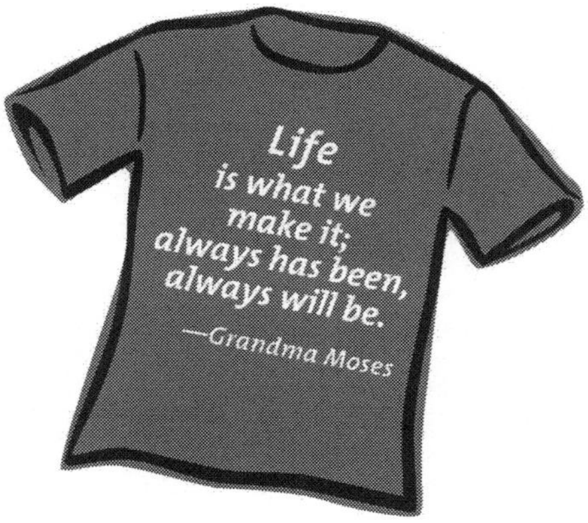
Life
is what we
make it;
always has been,
always will be.
—Grandma Moses

M

Q

R

S

U

V

W

Y

Z

Books For ALL Kinds of Readers

At ReadHowYouWant we understand that one size does not fit all types of readers. Our innovative, patent pending technology allows us to design new formats to make reading easier and more enjoyable for you. This helps improve your speed of reading and your comprehension. Our EasyRead printed books have been optimized to improve word recognition, ease eye tracking by adjusting word and line spacing as well as minimizing hyphenation. Our EasyRead SuperLarge editions have been developed to make reading easier and more accessible for vision-impaired readers. We offer Braille and DAISY formats of our books and all popular E-Book formats.

Made in United States
Orlando, FL
04 November 2026

90202362R00146